UNDERCOVER DESIRE
WHEN LOVE AND INTRIGUE COLLIDE IN

POLITICS

UNDERCOVER DESIRE

WHEN LOVE AND INTRIGUE COLLIDE IN POLITICS

ISABELLA

SAPPHIRE BOOKS

SALINAS, CALIFORNIA

Cover Design by Fineline
Editor - Heather Flornouy

Sapphire Books
Salinas, CA 93912
www.sapphirebooks.com

Printed in the United States of America
First edition – May 2024

work. The author retains all rights to use this work for purposes of generative AI training and development of any language learning system.

To the extent that the image on the cover of this book depicts a person or persons, such a person is merely a model and is not intended to portray any character feature in this book.

This and other Sapphire Books titles can be found at
www.sapphirebooks.com

Isabella's other books

Faithful Series
Always Faithful
Forever Faithful
Faithful Valor

American Yakuza Series
American Yakuza I
The Lies that Bind -American Yakuza II
Razor's Edge - American Yakuza III
Blood Honor: American Yakuza IV
American Yakuza - The Collection

ExecutiveSeries
Executive Disclosure
Surviving Reagan

Scarlet Series
Scarlet Masquerade
Scarlet Assassin

Stand Alone
Broken Shield
Dusty Road Home
Chasing Liberty
Cigar Barons: Blood isn't thicker than water, it's war.
The Gate
Twisted Deception: Love can be dangerous.

Short Stories
The Last Train
The Tinderella Chronicles: Big Sur Edition

Anthologies
Fandom to Fantasy: Volume 1
Fandom to Fantasy: Volume 2

Non-Fiction
A Beginner's Guide to Writing Lesbian Romance
A Beginner's Guide to Writing A Mystery Novel

Acknowledgements

To my editor, Heather Flournoy. You are so much more than my editor, you're a great friend.

To the readers who keep reading my stories. Thank you.

Dedication

To the love of my life.
May we always find the joy and laughter in everything
we do.

To my grandsons, Wesley and Rowan.

Chapter One

The soft hum of the campaign office filled Lexi's ears, punctuated by the rhythmic tap-tap-tapping of computer keys and the occasional murmur of hushed conversation. She sat at her desk, eyes narrowed in concentration as she scrutinized the latest polling data on her screen. Her brown hair was pulled back into a loose ponytail today, wisps framing her face as she leaned in closer to examine the numbers.

"Hey, Lexi." Ethan, the chief of staff for Congresswoman Marsh, approached her workspace. He took a long drag from his flavored vape pen before continuing, "We're getting some pushback on social media regarding the congresswoman's education policy. We need you to craft a response."

"Of course," Lexi replied without missing a beat. Her fingers flew across the keyboard, composing a concise rebuttal that highlighted the key points of the policy while simultaneously disarming the criticism. Before she hit send, she called Ethan over to look at the email.

"Nice work," Ethan commended, reading the response. "You always know how to make our message shine."

Lexi allowed herself a small smile. This was where her skills shined: navigating the complexities of political consulting.

"Thanks," Lexi responded, a hint of pride coloring her voice. "I just want to make sure we're putting our best foot forward."

"Speaking of which, I wanted to get your thoughts on this new ad concept." Ethan handed Lexi a storyboard for a potential TV spot. Her eyes scanned over the images and text, her mind already working through the implications and effectiveness of the proposed narrative.

"Interesting," she mused aloud, tapping her chin thoughtfully. "But what if we shifted the focus slightly? Emphasize the congresswoman's track record on job creation and economic growth instead of just her stance on taxes. Taxes are code for school bonds, and we don't want voters to get cringy on the school bond measures just yet. It would resonate more with voters who are concerned about their financial futures."

"Great idea," Ethan agreed, nodding appreciatively. "I'll pass that along to the creative team."

"Perfect." Lexi offered him a smile before diving back into her work with renewed determination.

Later that day, as evening shadows began to stretch across the busy office, Lexi found herself in an impromptu brainstorming session with Sarah, the press secretary. Together, they analyzed the latest news headlines and discussed strategies for shaping the upcoming week's media narrative.

"Congresswoman Marsh has been getting some flak for her position on immigration reform," Sarah said, concern creasing her brow. "Any ideas on how we can counteract that?"

After a moment of contemplation, Lexi suggested, "Why don't we highlight some individual stories of immigrants who have benefited from the congresswoman's policies? Humanize the issue and show how it positively impacts real people."

"Brilliant!" Sarah exclaimed, her eyes lighting up. "That will definitely resonate more with our audience."

"I think so," Lexi replied, warmth radiating through her chest at the knowledge that she was making a difference, one strategic decision at a time.

As the evening wore on, Lexi continued to navigate the ever-shifting political landscape with finesse and intelligence, her passion for her work never waning. And as the last rays of sunlight disappeared behind the horizon, she knew, without a doubt, that she was exactly where she was meant to be.

"Hey Lexi, we're all going for a drink. Wanna come?" Ethan said, scented vapor filling her office.

"I don't know," she said, looking around her desk. "I've still got a ton of work—"

"Lexi, if you're worried someone is going to sneak in here and do it, don't worry. It'll be here when you get back. Besides, it's been weeks since we have had a good laugh."

Lexi leaned back in her chair, raised her hands, clasped them together, and stretched. "I guess."

"That's the spirit. Let's go to the little pub around the corner."

Lexi grabbed her jacket, hit the lights, and threaded her arm through Ethan's. "Lead the way."

Half of the team was already seated around a round table littered with full beer glasses. Ethan patted a chair next to him and handed her a glass.

"Cheers," he said, raising his mug to the table.

A chorus of "Cheers" elevated the sound level in the pub and the frivolities began.

Ethan looked at Lexi and asked, "So, how's your love life?"

Lexi pressed her lips, together trying not to spit her beer out.

"Ethan," Sarah said. "Maybe she doesn't want you prying into her private life."

Lexi held up her hand, "It's okay." She smiled and looked at Ethan, the room suddenly quiet as everyone waited for her to answer. "It's simple. I'm married to my job, and I don't have time for a mistress. Besides, I'm way too focused on this campaign for a relationship."

"You know the ol' saying—all work and no play makes for a dull Lexi," Ethan said before sipping his beer.

"Ethan, how's your love life?" Lexi asked, figuring turnabout was fair play.

"Ethan also doesn't have time for a girlfriend," Sarah answered for him. "Besides, he hasn't met Ms. Right yet. Have you, Eth?" Sarah ruffled his hair.

"I'm holding out hope for the right woman." Ethan blushed.

Lexi had a sense early on that Ethan had a crush on her, bringing her coffee almost every morning, spending inordinate amounts of time sitting in the chair across from her desk discussing the latest political hanky-panky guised as political strategizing. Too often she'd had to remind him of her workload and the limited time she had. He reluctantly pushed off, vowing to be back before she knew it.

Gossip was the stock-in-trade of any political campaign. It frequently foreshadowed an impending crisis that left room for interpretation on both sides, so it was often used by the very political campaign it was targeted to hurt. Lexi was reminded of a particularly distasteful incident involving a congressman and his secret male lover, all designed to bring him out of the closet without him actually coming out. However, the clever congressman had been able to turn it on his political adversary, cornering him as a possible homophobe. His adversary spent the rest of the campaign ducking questions about his views of gay marriage instead of being able to focus on the issues that really mattered.

Very clever, indeed.

As everyone around the table continued to chat, Lexi looked at her watch. If she was lucky, she could get home in time to catch the late news, read a few chapters of her romance novel, gobble a bag of greasy chips, and finish that nice bottle of merlot she'd opened last night.

She wondered if it would be in bad taste to leave having only spent thirty minutes with the team.

Screw it.

"Alright, I'm off, guys. I've got a busy day tomorrow. So…" She finished her beer, stood, and slung her purse across her body. "I'll bid you good night and I…will see you all tomorrow."

A course of "good nights" followed her out of the pub.

"Lexi, Lexi." Ethan ran up to her. "I was wondering if you'd like to have dinner this weekend. I know this great little Greek—"

"Oh, gosh, Ethan. I'm sorry. I've made other plans. Maybe another time?"

"Of course, Yeah, I'm sorry. Bad idea."

"No, it's fine. I'm just…well, you know. Work, work, work."

"Yeah, no problem. Another time," he said over his shoulder as he made his way back into the pub.

She didn't have the heart to tell him that his plumbing didn't work with hers, but wasn't that why they called it a private life? To keep things private.

☙ ☙ ☙ ☙

Lexi looked at her bathroom mirror as she shrugged into a baby blue sweater. So much for doing her hair, she thought as it flew in all directions as she popped her head through.

"I don't know why I try," she said, puckering her lips and applying her lipstick. At least she'd remembered not to apply it before donning the sweater.

Her phone rang, the distinctive ringtone signaling it was her mom.

"Hey, Mom," she said, smiling. She and her mom were two cards—just in different decks.

"Hi, honey. Are you at work?"

Instinctively, she looked down at her watch. "No, I'm running a little behind. What's going on?"

"I was wondering if you wanted to have lunch. I haven't seen you in a month of Sundays, and I just wanted to catch up with my favorite daughter."

"Mom, I'm your only daughter." Lexi laughed.

"Yes, but you're still my favorite. I'm going to be down in your part of town for a meeting with an artist in one of those lofts above the warehouse district."

"Is that safe? Some of those buildings are sketchy."

"It's perfectly safe, sweetheart."

Lexi sighed. The gentrification of the area was one of the congresswoman's campaign talking points. People had their own spins on gentrification— it brought money into a depressed area; it forced longtime residents who probably couldn't afford to move to relocate; it changed the demographics, often displacing poorer residents and people of color. She'd heard it all. It was clear the congresswoman was walking a tight line on gentrification. Should she leave the poorer neighborhoods to fend for themselves, giving autonomy to the residents, or step in and bring a government solution to an already controversial issue? More government solutions meant government could hold it over the residents' heads, so she wanted to meet the movers and shakers to see how they could work toward bringing   money to the community through tax breaks while allowing the residents to keep their homes and benefit from the higher property values, have access to better options for food, and realize that the American Dream wasn't just for a select few.

"Sure, I'd love to have lunch. Wanna meet somewhere?" Lexi slung her bag across her chest and grabbed her keys. "Let's say eleven thirty?"

"How about Tobies?"

"Okay, Tobies it is. See you at lunch, Mom." Lexi locked her front door and made her way to her car.

"Love you, honey," her mom said, the background noise making it hard to hear.

The line went dead just as Lexi said, "Love you."

A sudden pang of guilt lanced through Lexi. If her mom was calling to schedule lunch, it meant she'd been lax in her daughterly duties. She loved spending time with her family, as they were her anchor in this constantly changing landscape of her life. Her mom filled her days with work and volunteering, and she made it a point to work in regular family barbecues . Probably where Lexi got her own time management skills, minus the family part. She had regularly promised to do better, and she would as soon as this campaign was over. Her brothers had figured out how to have a work-life balance, juggling kids, little league, and happy marriages. She would need to find someone first to even join them on that path.

"I'm sure this will be the topic of conversation with Mom," she whispered as she merged into slow traffic barely crawling down the expressway.

Lexi caught sight of a highway patrol officer leaning down at a car pulled off the side of the road. She was going slow enough to notice that the officer was female. She shivered with delight. She had a weakness for women in uniform, and it didn't really matter which uniform, especially if they filled it out like this highway patrol officer did. She watched the officer as she passed by, and then continued to do so in her rearview mirror.

She sighed.

Yep, she needed to get a girlfriend, or at least scratch that itch.

❦ ❦ ❦ ❦

Lexi, her sleeves rolled up and hair pulled back into a messy bun, leaned against a table strewn with papers, graphs, and brightly colored sticky notes. The mid-morning light spilled through the windows of Congresswoman Marsh's campaign headquarters, casting a warm glow and making it feel like the sun had specially chosen to spotlight their bustling office. Armed with this little boost of nature, she could barely contain her enthusiasm as she discussed the upcoming rally with Ethan.

He seemed a little aloof. Was he holding a grudge after being shot down at the pub? This was why she didn't date where she worked. It never went smoothly.

She shrugged. He'd get over it, but in the meantime, he needed to remember the pecking order. Or did she need to remember the pecking order? It didn't matter. The campaign would be over in a couple of weeks, and then they could talk about things later.

"Over a thousand people are expected to attend," Lexi said, excitement bubbling in her voice. "We need to make sure Congresswoman Marsh's message is clear and powerful. Our focus should be on healthcare reform and education—issues that resonate with our constituents."

Ethan nodded in agreement, his brow furrowed in concentration as he sucked on his vape pen. "Absolutely. We also need to emphasize how the congresswoman's policies will positively impact the community and create lasting change."

Lexi's heart swelled with pride as she thought about the difference they were making in the world, one campaign event at a time. She knew that their hard work would pay off, and that Congresswoman Marsh would continue to fight for the causes they all believed in. It was why she had agreed to come on board the campaign.

Lexi found herself surrounded by a sea of eager volunteers, hoping her energy was infectious as she rallied them for the upcoming event. She moved from group to group, offering words of encouragement and praise.

"Remember, you're not just handing out flyers or making phone calls," Lexi told them, her voice filled with conviction. "You're helping to shape the future of this country—for ourselves, our children, and our grandchildren. Every conversation you have, every door you knock on, could be the one that makes the difference."

Her words seemed to ignite a fire in the volunteers, each person visibly inspired by her passion and commitment. As Lexi looked around the room, she couldn't help but feel an overwhelming sense of gratitude and pride. These were the people who would help carry Congresswoman Marsh to victory, and she was honored to stand beside them in this fight.

As the day progressed, Lexi's heart raced with anticipation for tonight's event, a private fundraiser at an upscale restaurant. She knew that each person attending believed in Congresswoman Marsh's vision for a better world, and she couldn't wait to share her own enthusiasm and dedication with them. Besides, a fancy meal made working after hours better, didn't it?

"Lexi," Sarah called as she approached, her petite frame exuding confidence. "I need those poll numbers from the—"

"Hold that thought, Sarah," Lexi replied, looking down at her watch. "I gotta run, but we can discuss this when I get back." She smiled warmly. "If I don't hurry, my mom is going to kill me. See you all after lunch."

❧❧❧❧

"Hey, Mom," Lexi said, bending down to place a kiss on her cheek.

"Hey, honey. I'm so happy to see you." Cynthia's eyes lit up. "Can you have a glass of wine?" Her mom motioned the waiter over. "Can we get..." Cynthia looked over at Lexi.

"Iced tea. I have to go back to work later," she said with a wink to the waiter as she tucked the napkin on her lap and reached for a bread roll. "Oh, and water too. Thank you." She sighed and looked at her mom. "Everything okay? Is Dad okay?"

"He's fine. You know your father, workaholic, his usual golf game every Saturday. Not much changes on that front."

"Workaholic, that's the pot calling the kettle..." Lexi let it hang out there.

"Yes, yes, I know."

"You okay, Mom?" Something seemed off with her mom, but she couldn't quite put her finger on it.

Her heart raced as she noticed tears in her mom's eyes. She slid over to her mom's side of the table and wrapped her in a hug. "What's wrong?"

"Cancer."

She collapsed inward, as if she'd been punched in the stomach. Everything rolled to a screeching stop as she fought back a sudden anxiety attack. "What? What kind of cancer?"

Her mom patted her hand and straightened up. "Breast. They think it's not very aggressive, so there's probably nothing to worry about."

"Mom? I want you to get a second opinion. What does Dad say? What's next?"

"Slow down, honey. Your father doesn't know."

"Why?"

"He's so busy at work, and since the doctor said they've caught it early, I don't want him to worry. I just needed to tell someone, and frankly, I don't want my business on blast. I just couldn't handle the pitiful stares and the whispering behind my back."

Her father worry? Never. He was a get up, wipe some dirt on it, and keep going kinda guy. She couldn't remember the last time her dad actually worried about anything. Now her mother, that was a different story.

"Mom, this isn't an affair or something, where those biddies have something to gossip about. This is life changing."

"No, no it's not. I've got an appointment with the oncologist and we're going to come up with a game plan."

"I'm coming."

Cynthia covered her daughter's hands with her own. "I'm a big girl, Lexi. I got this."

Lexi slumped back against the booth. "Jesus, Mom."

"Sweetheart, I'm sorry. I should've just kept my big mouth shut. Seriously, it's going to be okay. I promise."

"I don't care, I want to be there." Lexi squeezed her mother tighter. "Do the boys know?"

"Absolutely not. They'll just tell your father and then, well…"

"You don't think Dad deserves to know? I mean depending on the treatment, you could be looking at surgery, chemo, I don't know what else. You think you'll be able to hide it if your hair falls out?"

Cynthia reached up and touched her hair. "You don't think…"

"Your hair or your life. Let's go with your life. Hair grows back, Mom."

"I know, but…" Her mom eased her head back and blew out a long, deep breath. Her mom's signature way of dealing with bad news was to not really deal with it at all. Lexi was surprised she actually told her about the cancer.

Cancer.

Now that was a gut punch. And the only way to counter a gut punch was to fight back. Hard.

"I'm going to talk to Congresswoman Marsh and see about getting some time off."

"Absolutely not. I won't hear of it, Alexandra."

"But, Mom—"

Cynthia put up her hand. The subject was officially closed.

"I'm starving. Let's order."

Their conversation weaved back and forth from Cynthia's gallery shows, to Lexi's brother, to her job. Her mother was the depository of all familial information, and Lexi usually told her mother anything she didn't want to tell her dad. Her mom was the filter and usually softened the blow when Cynthia informed Lexi's dad of any bad news.

"Let's get a cappuccino at that cute little coffee shop down the street," Cynthia said, hoisting her oversized purse up.

Lexi looked at her watch. A coffee would make her late, but she didn't feel right about leaving her mother at the moment. "Sure, I'd love to spend more time with my mom."

"Are you being funny or serious? I mean, if you have to get back to work, I'll understand."

Lexi threaded her arm through her mom's and pulled   her toward the door. "I'm serious. Let's have coffee."

The realization of how fragile life was shook Lexi to her core. She wasn't about to let her mom travel that path alone. She'd have to tell Congresswoman Marsh as soon as possible, to prep her for when she would need to have time off for her mom's treatments.

The cool breeze wrapped itself around the two women walking arm in arm and felt good after sitting in the stuffy restaurant.

"So, anyone new in your love life?"

"Mom." Lexi shook her head.

"I met this really nice girl at the dentist office the other day. I was talking about you, and she seemed really interested."

"Mom, she's probably just being nice."

Lexi and her mother stood at the counter considering their coffee options.

"Cappuccino, Chai latte, mocha latte," Her mom rattled off the menu as the line behind them grew. "Well, she seemed really interested in my daughter when I told her that you were listed in that magazine with the most up-and-coming lesbians in politics."

"Mom," Lexi whispered, lowering her head.

"What?" Cynthia lowered her head and whispered, "Isn't it okay to say lesbian?"

"Mom, please." Lexi gave her mom an imploring look, paid for their drinks, turned, and promptly face-planted right into the chest of a police officer.

Stepping back, she blushed and said, "I am so sorry, Officer. I should have watched where I was going."

Lexi looked up and instantly recognized the female officer from the traffic stop earlier on her way to work.

A wry smile eased across the officer's face as she looked down and said, "No harm."

Lexi's heart raced as she looked at the nameplate on her chest that was eye level for Lexi.

Church.

"Thank you, Officer Church. Perhaps, I can buy you a coffee?"

"That won't be necessary, ma'am."

Lexi's knees weakened slightly at the low, dulcet

tone of the woman's voice. "Well, again, my apologies." Lexi said, sidestepping around the officer.

Her mother pulled her to the waiting area. "Oh, now she's cute."

Lexi straightened up, suddenly self-conscious. "Mom, please." She felt a blush crawl up her cheeks as she spied the officer placing her order.

Wow, she was gorgeous. Her body armor fit her like a glove. Razor pleats, a generous curve of her hips, and Lexi could imagine...

Stop, Lexi told herself.

Maybe she should pass her a business card. No, that would be too presumptuous, wouldn't it? Lexi nervously licked her lower lip just as the officer looked her way.

The officer turned away to continue chatting with the barista, and Lexi hoped that kept her from seeing the embarrassment that surely painted her face.

As soon as Lexi's name was called, she grabbed their coffee and made her way past Officer Church toward the door. She thought she saw a slight glance and smile in her direction from the highway patrolwoman, but Lexi was racing to get out of the coffee shop before her mother could embarrass her further.

Chapter Two

The sun dipped beyond the horizon, leaving the city bathed in hues of pink and gold. Lexi positioned herself at the window of her cramped office, hands resting on her hips. As her gaze scanned the lively streets below, a resolute determination washed over her.

Anticipation lingered thick in the air as Lexi navigated the dimly lit campaign headquarters. Her pulse echoed with the rhythmic tick of the wall clock, time slowing to a crawl as she awaited the crucial poll numbers. Fingers drummed incessantly against her thigh, a silent plea for favorable results.

"Come on, come on," she murmured, the room echoing with her restless impatience.

"Lexi, relax. You're making me nervous." Sarah's strained voice seemed to be attempting reassurance.

"Sorry, I just…this is it. These are the moments we've been working toward," Lexi replied, seeking to steady her breathing.

"Whatever happens, we've given it our all," Ethan chimed in, his eyes fixed on the incoming data.

"Agreed." Lexi nodded, swallowing hard. "But it sure would be nice to see some tangible results."

Silence thickened as they waited, the tension palpable. Suddenly, numbers materialized on the screen, and Lexi felt her heart surge into her throat.

"Guys, look!" she exclaimed, pointing at the display. "Congresswoman Marsh's approval rating is up by six percent!"

"Wow, that's amazing!" Sarah cried, excitement widening her eyes.

"Fantastic work, everyone," Ethan added, beaming with pride.

"But we can't let up now," Lexi reminded them. "These numbers are promising, but we need to keep pushing forward."

"Agreed," Sarah said firmly. "What's our next move?"

"Let's brainstorm fresh ideas for more media coverage," Lexi suggested, her mind already racing with possibilities. "We need to capitalize on this momentum."

"Great idea," Ethan said. "I'll reach out to our contacts and see if we can get Congresswoman Marsh booked on some talk shows."

"Perfect. And Sarah, can you draft a press release highlighting the congresswoman's recent increase in poll numbers?"

"Of course." Sarah's fingers were already flying across her keyboard.

As the team mobilized, Lexi felt exhilaration surge through her veins. They were effecting change, steering the course of the election. Yet, as the night wore on, an eerie unease crept in, a nagging sense that unseen forces conspired against them. It felt like the calm before a storm, and Lexi did not like it one bit.

"Lexi, are you alright?" Ethan asked, his brow furrowed with concern.

"I'm not sure," she admitted, her voice barely a whisper. "I just have this unsettling feeling..."

"Trust your instincts," he said. "If something feels off, there might be a reason for it."

"Let's regroup in the morning and reassess our strategy," Lexi suggested, her eyes scanning the darkened office. "We need to be prepared for anything that comes our way."

"Sounds like a plan," Sarah said, her own expression shadowed with uncertainty.

≈∿≈∿

The morning sun filtered through the blinds, casting slivers of light across Lexi's face as she sat in Congresswoman Marsh's office. The scent of freshly brewed coffee mingled with the faint aroma of leather-bound books lining the walls. A hushed murmur of activity echoed from the corridors outside, a stark contrast to the previous night's frenzy.

"Lexi," Congresswoman Marsh began, her voice smooth yet commanding. "I need you to dig deeper into our opponent's past. We need something that will make the voters think twice about him."

"Understood, Congresswoman," Lexi replied, tapping her pen against her notepad and hiding the concern that she felt brewing in her gut. She knew that delving into their opponent's history could be a dangerous game, but it was crucial to their campaign's success. All campaigns did oppo research, but because of the spin doctors every campaign also had on staff, the chance that the oppo research Marsh's team dug up could come back to bite *them* in the ass was reasonably high. So, both the research itself and its deployment had to be done intelligently—clean, meticulous, and as covert as possible.

"Anything we can use to discredit him would be

invaluable," Congresswoman Marsh continued, her gaze locked onto Lexi's. Her unwavering determination was palpable. "We can't let Dan Brown get away with his underhanded tactics."

"Of course, ma'am," Lexi assured her, her fingers already itching to uncover any hidden skeletons. Her mind raced with possibilities, strategies, and potential risks. This was the part of her job that excited her most— the thrill of the hunt. It was almost like searching for the perfect woman, if she even existed.

"Good," Marsh said with a curt nod. "I trust you'll find something."

"I'll do my best," Lexi promised.

As she left the office, Lexi passed Ethan in the hallway. He leaned against the wall, puffing on his vape pen, a cloud of sweet-scented smoke dissipating around him.

"Find anything juicy yet?" he asked, quirking an eyebrow.

"Only that smoke." She laughed. "Working on it." A wry smile played on her lips. "You know I love a challenge."

"Let me know if you need any help," Ethan offered, his tone both teasing and sincere.

"Will do," she said, already envisioning the web of deceit that lay before her. She felt a thrill of anticipation, tempered by a nagging sense of unease. Uncovering secrets was exhilarating, but it also had the potential to blow up in your face if you weren't careful.

As Lexi settled into her workspace, she immersed herself in research, sifting through articles, social media posts, and archived documents. With each click, she delved deeper into Dan Brown's past, searching for any hint of scandal or impropriety.

Hours ticked away as Lexi pieced together fragments of information, her fingers dancing across the keyboard. The hum of activity around her faded into the background, drowned out by her relentless pursuit of the truth.

"Lexi." Sarah's voice broke through her concentration. "You've been at this for hours. Are you okay?"

Pausing, Lexi realized just how tense her shoulders had become, her eyes strained from staring at the screen. "Yeah," she admitted with a sigh. "I can't shake the feeling that something big is lurking out there. Something we're not seeing."

"Keep digging," Sarah said, her sharp smile conveying both empathy and determination. "We need an edge to win this."

"Thanks, Sarah," Lexi replied, grateful for the support. "I can assure you I won't stop until I find it." She offered a small smile and continued her search, her mind racing with possibilities and her heart pounding in her chest. "Dan Brown," she muttered under her breath, her eyes narrowing. "You have no idea what's coming for you."

❧ ❧ ❧ ❧

Lexi's eyes scanned the faces before her. "I appreciate your dedication to Congresswoman Marsh's cause. What I need from you is any information or rumors you've come across regarding Dan Brown. Anything at all could be useful."

The volunteers from a diverse slice of life—college students, people running businesses from home, retirees—exchanged glances, a murmur of conversation rising among them. Lexi listened intently, her heart thumping in her chest as she hoped for a vital clue.

"Actually," a young woman said, raising her hand. "I did overhear something at my college campus the other day. Some people were talking about how Dan Brown's been seen with this shady guy who has connections to the drugs scene."

"Interesting," Lexi murmured, her pulse quickening. "Did you catch a name?"

"Jose Guevara, I think," the volunteer supplied nervously. "His guys are all over campus selling drugs."

"Thank you," Lexi said, her mind racing with possibilities. She didn't want to press the college student further and have her thinking she was in her business, but...well, it was something, at least, and gave her a starting point on Brown. "That's excellent."

"Keep up the good work, everyone," she continued. "We'll get more info on him and win this for Congresswoman Marsh."

As she walked away from the group, Lexi felt a mixture of elation and unease. Was she on the verge of uncovering something monumental? Or was she stepping into dangerous territory that could threaten everything she'd worked for?

Either way, there was only one way to find out. As her eyes narrowed, Lexi resolved to follow the lead to its conclusion, no matter the cost.

Chapter Three

Maxine "Max" Church gripped the steering wheel of her Highway Patrol cruiser, her knuckles turning white as she navigated the busy highway. The hum of engines and the rush of traffic were a familiar soundtrack to her days, but it was the silence in between that she sought—the moments when her intuition sharpened and she sensed something amiss on the road.

Her eyes scanned the sea of vehicles, darting from one to another like a hawk surveying its prey. Max was a force to be reckoned with; her tall stature and athletic build commanded attention and respect from those around her. With short hair framing her piercing eyes, there was an air of determination and authority in every line of her face.

As she patrolled the congested lanes, Max's mind wandered to the people behind the wheels of these machines. She had come across all kinds—from law-abiding citizens to reckless drivers who endangered the lives of others. But it was her unwavering sense of duty and responsibility that kept her focused on her mission: to ensure the safety of her community.

The sun cast a golden glow on the blacktop, its warmth a sharp contrast to the coolness of Max's demeanor. Despite the heat outside, she remained collected and alert, a testament to her discipline honed during her time in the army. Her tactical abilities had served her well then, and now they made her an asset to the Highway Patrol.

Max's gaze fell upon a vehicle speeding through traffic, its driver clearly disregarding the safety of others. Her breath hitched, and for a brief moment, her world narrowed to the single goal of reining in the offender. She immediately hit the siren and pulled out of her hiding spot, weaving through traffic to catch up. As she pursued the car, she couldn't help but wonder what awaited her this time—another routine stop, or something more? In today's world, you never knew what you would walk up on.

It was in moments like these that Max felt most alive, her heart pounding in her chest as adrenaline coursed through her veins. She knew that every interaction held the potential for conflict, yet she approached each one with grace and composure.

"Control your emotions," she whispered to herself, a mantra borne from years of experience. Max was not one to let her guard down, especially when it came to protecting those around her. It was this unwavering dedication to her role as a highway patrol officer that made her stand out among her peers.

The speeding car finally pulled over, and as Max stepped out of her cruiser, she couldn't help but feel a sense of pride. Pride in her work, in her commitment to upholding the law, and in the person she had become. For Max, there was no greater honor than serving and protecting her community, even if it meant confronting danger head-on.

"Let's see what we've got here," she murmured under her breath, steeling herself for the encounter ahead. With measured strides, she ran her fingers down the side of the vehicle, leaving her fingerprints on it in the event the encounter went sideways. She approached the driver's window, her tall figure casting an imposing shadow on the driver.

She put on her best professional smile and took note of the young man inside. He looked nervous, tapping his fingers on the wheel.

"Is there a problem, Officer?" the young man asked, trying to sound confident but failing miserably.

Max's voice was calm and even. "You were going a bit over the speed limit back there. Can I see your license, registration and your insurance card, please?"

The driver handed them over, and Max quickly scanned each one, making sure everything was in order. As she did so, she couldn't help but notice the sweat forming on the young man's forehead.

"Is everything alright?" she asked, sensing his discomfort.

"Uh, y-yeah," he stuttered. "Just wasn't paying attention, you know?"

Max nodded, knowing full well that everyone had their reasons for breaking the law. She leaned in slightly, studying the driver's face for any signs of drugs or alcohol.

She returned her attention to the driver's documents, noting the faint wear at the edges of the license and scrutinizing the registration for any discrepancies.

"Mr. Thompson," Max said, finally looking up from the papers in her hand. "Can you tell me why you were driving above the speed limit?"

The driver, a young man with an unkempt appearance, shifted uncomfortably in his seat before responding. "I wasn't going that fast," he mumbled, avoiding eye contact.

"I clocked you at ninety-two miles an hour. Speeding is dangerous and puts other drivers at risk," Max reminded him sternly. She paused momentarily, allowing her words to sink in, before continuing. "Is there a reason you felt the need to drive so fast?"

Unprepared for Max's question, the driver's face twisted into a sneer as he spat out, "What's it to you, dyke?"

Inwardly, Max bristled at the insult, but she maintained her composure as she looked him straight in the eye. Though it would have been easy to let anger cloud her judgment, she chose instead to channel her energy into enforcing the law with dignity and professionalism.

"Your choice of language is inappropriate and, quite frankly, I find it offensive," Max curtly informed the driver. "My job is to ensure the safety of everyone on the road, and that includes reckless behavior such as speeding."

The driver scoffed, but Max could see the unease behind his bravado. He knew he was in the wrong, and her calm and assertive demeanor only served to reinforce that fact.

Max had intended to let the driver off with a warning, but his cruel remark had crossed a line. She decided that a speeding ticket was in order. As she filled out the citation, her mind raced. Part of her wanted to lash out at the man's bigotry, but she knew better than to let her emotions dictate her actions. Instead, she focused on maintaining her professionalism and upholding the law.

Walking back, she leaned down. "Here is your ticket for exceeding the speed limit," Max said firmly as she handed the document through the window. "I strongly advise you to be more cautious on the road."

The driver snarled at her, his face contorted with rage. "You're just another power-tripping dyke," he spat, tossing the ticket onto the passenger seat.

Max took a deep breath and bit the inside of her mouth, steadying herself against the surge of annoyance that threatened to unravel her composure. This wasn't the first time she'd faced such blatant disrespect, nor would it be the last. But she refused to let this man's ignorance undermine her dedication to her job. Her eyes locked with his, unyielding and resolute.

"Sir, I warn you, any further abusive language or aggressive behavior won't be tolerated," she said calmly. "I am simply doing my job, which is to enforce traffic laws and ensure the safety of everyone on the road."

The driver glared at her, his knuckles white on the steering wheel, but he held his tongue. He seemed to recognize that pushing her further would only exacerbate the situation.

"Look," she said gently but firmly, leaning down to his level so that her eyes met his gaze directly. "I understand this isn't what you wanted today, but driving at those speeds puts at risk not only your life, but also the lives of others."

The driver sneered, clearly uninterested in her words, but Max pressed on. "Take this as a wake-up call, and try to be more responsible behind the wheel in the future. It's not just about the ticket or the points on your license. It's about making sure everyone gets home safely."

"Fuck you," he said as he raised his window, put the car in drive, and sped off.

Max shook her head, waving away the dust kicked up by the rapid departure. As she returned to her patrol car, she couldn't help but feel a sense of duty and responsibility weigh upon her shoulders. Even though she knew she couldn't reach everyone, each encounter like this one made her question her dedication to her job. While she wanted to ensure the safety of her community, she also had to come to terms that the community was changing and the public's attitude toward policing had done a one-eighty in recent years. Every traffic stop brought with it a very real risk that she might not go home.

While her heart raced with the adrenaline that came from handling a difficult situation, Max knew she couldn't afford to dwell on it. There were still miles to cover, countless drivers to protect, and a world beyond the confines of the highway that needed her. She allowed herself a deep breath, centering her thoughts before starting the engine and merging back onto the busy road.

"Stay focused, Max," she whispered to herself, her fingers tightening around the steering wheel. "You've got a job to do, and people counting on you."

Chapter Four

L exi was finally going to enjoy her first day off in weeks, and she planned on doing just that. She drove down the highway, her mind buzzing with anticipation for what awaited her at home. She'd just left the sex shop with a little black bag filled with toys that she couldn't wait to try out. The thought made her blush and grin in equal measure.

The sound of a siren pierced the afternoon, and Lexi's heart jumped into her throat. Panic washed over her as she glanced in the rearview mirror, only to see the flashing red and blue lights of a patrol car behind her. Her palms went clammy on the steering wheel as she tried to remember the last time she'd been pulled over.

"Get it together, Lexi," she muttered under her breath, scanning the road for a safe place to pull over. As she maneuvered her car toward the shoulder, her thoughts raced with the potential consequences of this unexpected encounter. She'd always prided herself on being calm and collected, but tonight was different— she felt vulnerable and exposed, a sensation she loathed.

As Lexi came to a stop, she took several deep breaths, attempting to steady her nerves as she eyed the cruiser in the rearview mirror. It wasn't until the officer emerged from the vehicle that Lexi realized just how nervous she truly was.

The officer approached her car with a sense of purpose, her expression serious and professional. The crisp lines of her uniform accentuated her athletic build, and her short hair framed her face in a way that seemed both practical and stylish. Lexi couldn't help but notice the confident way she carried herself, her every movement measured and precise. She pulled her sunglasses off and tucked an end into her chest pocket. That's when Lexi noticed her name, Church.

Fuck my life, Lexi thought as she remembered their brief encounter at the coffee shop.

The officer's stern voice cut through the tension. Lexi felt her anxiety spike. "License, registration, and proof of insurance, please," she demanded, her hand outstretched. Lexi instantly recognized the smooth, low tone.

"Y-yes, of course," Lexi stammered, her hands trembling as she rummaged through the glove compartment for her registration and insurance card. She could feel the heat of Officer Church's gaze on her, a formidable presence that seemed to seep into her very skin. Her heart pounded heavily in her chest as she realized, with growing dread, that her license was missing.

"Officer, I-I must've left my license at…uh, the store I just visited," Lexi confessed, feeling her face flush with embarrassment. She didn't dare divulge the nature of the boutique, which seemed inappropriate, given the circumstances. She handed the officer her insurance and registration.

"Ma'am, you should always carry your license while driving," Officer Church reprimanded, her voice firm and authoritative. Her eyes bore into Lexi, seeming to pierce her very soul. She looked at the cards Lexi had handed her.

"I know, I'm so sorry. I promise it won't happen

again," Lexi said, desperate to defuse the situation. She tried to swallow the lump forming in her throat but found it nearly impossible. "I was just on my way home to enjoy a much-deserved day off..." Lexi hesitated, debating whether to continue or not. "I was just excited to get home safely and probably overcompensated."

"Excitement is no excuse for negligence, ma'am," Officer Church responded, her tone unwavering. Lexi winced inwardly at the officer's words, knowing they were true yet wishing she could somehow escape this predicament unscathed.

"Please let me explain." Lexi knew she was grasping at straws, but she was desperate to curtail any further embarrassment in front of the gorgeous Officer Church. "I didn't realize I was driving too slow." She bit her lip, hoping her honesty might elicit some sympathy.

"Slow driving can be just as dangerous as speeding, ma'am," Officer Church said, her expression softening ever so slightly. "However, I appreciate your candor."

Lexi noticed Officer Church's eyes narrow as she studied her more closely, her gaze flicking from the woman's trembling hands to the beads of sweat forming on her forehead. Did she recognize Lexi from the coffee shop? "Ma'am, are you feeling alright? Your pupils seem rather dilated."

"Um, I'm okay," Lexi stammered, her heart rate quickening under the officer's scrutiny. She couldn't believe this was happening. All she wanted was to enjoy her day off in peace! "Too much coffee, I'm sure." Lexi hoped that the officer understood the reference.

"Are you sure?" Officer Church questioned, her tone laced with suspicion. "You seem...off." Her keen observation skills were evident as she scanned Lexi's appearance for any signs of impairment.

"Really, I'm fine," Lexi insisted, though her voice quivered slightly. "I guess I'm just nervous because I can't remember the last time I was pulled over."

"Regardless, I need you to step out of the car, if you don't mind," Officer Church commanded, making it clear that Lexi actually had zero choice in the matter.

Lexi's stomach dropped like a stone, and panic clawed at her insides at the thought of the officer searching her car and discovering the black bag and its contents.

"Of course," Lexi replied, her voice barely above a whisper. She knew better than to argue with a police officer, especially one as formidable as Church. As she opened the car door and stepped onto the pavement, her legs felt like jelly beneath her.

"Place your hands on your head, please," Church instructed, watching Lexi closely.

Swallowing hard, Lexi complied, her palms sweaty and her heart thudding wildly in her chest. She felt like a criminal even though she hadn't done anything wrong. And yet, the embarrassment she felt at the prospect of being caught with the items in her black bag made her feel as though she had something to hide.

"Spread your legs shoulder-width apart," Officer Church said, and Lexi obeyed, struggling to keep her balance on shaky limbs.

As the officer began her inspection, Lexi's thoughts raced, a chaotic whirlwind of fear and humiliation. She couldn't help but wonder what would happen when Officer Church discovered the black bag. Would she be arrested? Fined? Or worse? It was absolutely ridiculous, of course, because there was nothing illegal about her purchase, but the thoughts just would not stop.

"Keep still, Miss Anders," Officer Church admonished gently as Lexi trembled. "I'm just doing my job."

"I know," Lexi whispered, shutting her eyes tightly against the tears threatening to spill over. "It's just...I've never been in this kind of situation before."

"Try to relax," Officer Church advised, her voice softer now. "If you have nothing to hide, there's no reason to be afraid."

But Lexi couldn't shake the feeling that she was about to be exposed—in more ways than one—and the shame that came with it was nearly unbearable. As her mind continued to race with questions and anxieties, a glimmer of hope emerged. Perhaps Officer Church held some hidden empathy, buried beneath her hardened exterior. And maybe, just maybe, that empathy could be her saving grace.

"Do you mind if I search your car?"

"Um, sure. I guess." Lexi fidgeted and sighed. "Is this really necessary?"

"Well, your driving gave me suspicion to pull you over. I could call out a canine. If you prefer." Church stared hard at Lexi.

"No, that's fine. Do what you need to do." Now she just wanted the situation to be over.

"Stay where you are, Miss Anders," Officer Church ordered, her gaze never leaving Lexi as she approached the passenger's door. With a gloved hand, she opened it slowly, carefully, and then stepped back to allow Lexi a clear view of her actions.

Lexi couldn't tear her eyes away from the scene unfolding before her. Her heart pounded in her chest, each beat a painful reminder of the increasing humiliation that lay just beyond her control. She watched as Officer Church began her methodical search, her fingers deftly moving through the contents of her glove box, then the center console, and finally coming to rest on the black bag that sat innocently on the passenger seat.

"Is this yours, Miss Anders?" she asked, lifting the bag with an air of detached curiosity. Lexi swallowed hard, nodding her head in affirmation. "May I look inside?"

"Uh, yes, of course," Lexi stammered, struggling to maintain her composure. "Go ahead."

Officer Church's fingers worked efficiently at the drawstring, and Lexi braced herself for the wave of embarrassment that would inevitably follow. The officer pulled out one item after another, placing them delicately on the trunk of Lexi's car as if they were fragile pieces of evidence in some kind of twisted crime scene. Each piece seemed to taunt her, mocking her very existence.

"Interesting," Officer Church murmured, her expression unreadable as she examined each object. Lexi felt the heat rise in her cheeks, her ears burning with shame. She willed herself to remain calm, but her thoughts spiraled into chaos, a cacophony of doubts and fears assaulting her psyche.

"Is there a problem, Officer?" Lexi ventured hesitantly, her voice barely audible above the sound of her own heartbeat.

"Miss Anders," Officer Church began, her tone measured and controlled. "It is not my place to judge the personal preferences of others, but I must remind you that it is crucial to keep your full attention on the road while driving. Your slow driving aroused my suspicion, and I am obligated to investigate any potential dangers."

The corners of Officer Church's mouth twitched upward ever so slightly as she gazed upon the array of toys displayed on Lexi's trunk. Even in her most dire moments, Lexi couldn't help but notice how this subtle hint of amusement softened the otherwise stern officer's features.

Putting the items back in the bag, Officer Church asked, "Do you have any identification on you?"

Lexi remembered her campaign badge tucked in her shirt. Pulling it free, she flashed it at Officer Church. "Will this work?"

Inspecting it closer, Officer Church asked, "You work for Congresswoman Marsh?"

"I do."

"Hmm, well I'll let you off with a warning this time. But watch your speed and try to stay with the flow of traffic."

Lexi could feel the heat rising in her cheeks as she stammered out an apology. "Y-Yes, Officer. I'm sorry for my slow driving. It won't happen again."

"See that it doesn't," the officer replied, her tone firm yet not unkind. She began to gather the items from atop the trunk, placing them one by one back into the black bag with a deliberate slowness that made Lexi squirm. Once everything was securely inside, she handed the bag to Lexi, who took it with trembling hands. Their eyes met, and for a moment Lexi couldn't breathe. She held Church's steely stare with an intense gaze of her own and felt a wave of arousal like a lightning bolt had struck the air around her, electricity buzzing everywhere.

Officer Church blinked, and it was like her eyes

came back into sharp focus. She blinked again, then broke eye contact.

"Drive safely, Miss Anders." With those final words, Officer Church returned to her patrol car, leaving Lexi standing there, her heart pounding and her mind a whirlwind of emotions. Relief washed over her like cool water, but confusion gnawed at her thoughts. Why had she been let off without even a citation?

Climbing back into her car, Lexi set the bag down on the passenger seat and started the engine. As she pulled away from the roadside, her mind raced with questions about Officer Church's actions. It wasn't just the fact that she'd been let go without a ticket. Something about the way the officer had looked at her stirred an excitement that had nothing at all to do with fear.

Chapter Five

Max leaned forward in her patrol car, her fingers drumming lightly on the steering wheel as she thought back to the traffic stop with Lexi Anders. The evening sun dipped below the horizon, casting long shadows across the asphalt. Her mind's eye conjured up the image of Lexi's flushed cheeks as Max methodically inspected each item from the black bag. She recognized the woman from the coffee shop as soon as she walked up to the car. Now she had a name to go with the beautiful face.

Max played the interaction over again in her head.

"Interesting collection you have here," Max had commented, holding up a particularly unusual-looking toy. Her professionalism never wavered, and she made sure to scrutinize each object with the same care she would've given any other piece of evidence.

"Uh, yeah...I guess so," Lexi had replied, her voice barely audible over the hum of passing cars.

Max could feel the tension rolling off her in waves, her own heart thudding against her rib cage as she tried to maintain her composure. She had seen many strange things during her time as a highway patrol officer, but this encounter was proving more difficult to shake off than most. It wasn't just the contents of the bag that fascinated her—it was the woman herself, Lexi Anders, who seemed caught between embarrassment and defiance.

"Everything seems to be in order," Max had said finally, setting the last item back into the black bag and tying it shut. She couldn't help but steal another glance at Lexi, trying to read the emotions flickering across her expressive face.

"Thank you, Officer," Lexi had murmured, her eyes meeting Max's for a brief, charged moment before darting away again. "I appreciate your, um, thoroughness."

"Of course, ma'am. Just doing my job." Max had nodded, her own cheeks warming at the unexpected compliment.

"Damn it," Max muttered under her breath, shaking her head as she tried to refocus on the task at hand. She had a job to do, and she couldn't afford to let her curiosity about Lexi Anders—or the contents of that black bag—distract her from her duties.

"Get it together, Church," she admonished herself, taking a deep breath and gripping the steering wheel more firmly. The road stretched out before her, an endless ribbon of asphalt that led toward the next traffic stop, the next encounter, and, perhaps, another chance to cross paths with Lexi Anders.

"Control, this is Unit two-oh-six reporting back on duty," Max spoke into her radio, her voice steady despite the turmoil of emotions brewing within her.

"Copy that, Unit two-oh-six," the dispatcher responded.

As Max drove through the quiet streets, her thoughts were consumed by the encounter with Lexi. She couldn't help but feel a pang of sympathy for the young woman, knowing all too well the humiliation she must have experienced during the inspection. It was never easy having one's personal life exposed to a stranger, especially under such circumstances.

"Stop it, Max," she chastised herself, shaking her head as if to clear her thoughts. "You were just doing your job."

But even as she tried to rationalize her actions, she wondered why Lexi Anders was *so* nervous. Was she hiding something? Or just naturally jittery? And, perhaps most importantly, why did Max find herself so affected by their brief interaction? First the coffee shop and now the traffic stop.

"Focus," she whispered, forcing her attention back to the road. "You've got a job to do."

As the miles passed beneath her tires, Max found herself reflecting on her own experiences. She knew what it was like to be vulnerable, to have her secrets laid bare for others to see. It wasn't something she wished upon anyone, let alone someone who seemed as kindhearted as Lexi. She remembered Lexi offering to buy her coffee as an apology for bumping into her.

"Maybe I should have handled it differently," Max thought, her brow furrowing as she considered her options. "But what would have been the right way to handle it? The law is the law."

Her mind raced with possibilities, each scenario playing out in vivid detail as she tried to find a solution that would ease her conscience. But with every imagined outcome, Max was left feeling even more conflicted than before.

"Damn it," she muttered under her breath, her frustration mounting. "Why am I letting this get to me?"

But deep down, she knew the answer. It wasn't just about Lexi, it was about the power dynamics at play, the fine line between duty and humanity that Max walked every day as an officer of the law.

"Maybe...Maybe I need to find a balance, or at least a girlfriend," Max mused, her grip on the steering wheel loosening slightly as she allowed herself to entertain the idea.

And as she continued to drive into the night, the image of Lexi's emerald eyes lingered in the back of her mind. A reminder that sometimes, the most powerful connections were forged in the most unlikely of circumstances.

Chapter Six

L exi exhaled deeply as she watched Officer Church's patrol car drive away. Her heart continued to race, but relief washed over her as she realized that she'd managed to evade a ticket after their second encounter. She rubbed her palms against her jeans, trying to wipe off the residual sweat from the tense exchange.

"Can't believe I dodged that bullet," Lexi muttered to herself, her eyes still locked on the receding tail lights . She glanced down at the empty passenger seat next to her, half expecting to find a citation placed there. But there was nothing but her black bag. Confusion furrowed her brow as she turned her gaze back to the road.

Why would Officer Church let me go without issuing a ticket? Lexi wondered, her thoughts churning like a whirlpool. The officer had been firm and resolute during their conversation, and it didn't make sense for her just to let Lexi go with a warning. There had to be something more to it.

"Maybe she recognized me from the campaign?" Lexi pondered aloud, her voice barely audible over the hum of the car's engine. "No, no, that doesn't seem likely." Her mind raced through various scenarios, each one less plausible than the last. She couldn't shake the feeling that there was an underlying reason behind Officer Church's decision, one that eluded her grasp.

As she drove on, Lexi replayed the interaction

in her head, searching for clues. She recalled Officer Church's steely eyes, her athletic build that hinted at a possible military connection, and her sexy short hair that framed her face with determination. Lexi found herself strangely drawn to the officer, despite their brief and somewhat hostile meeting.

"Get a grip, Lexi," she chastised herself, shaking off the unexpected attraction. "You need to focus on the campaign, not the enigmatic cop who let you off the hook."

But despite her best efforts to distract herself, Lexi's thoughts circled back to Officer Church like a moth to a flame. She couldn't help but wonder what lay beneath that resolute exterior—and why she had been spared from receiving a ticket.

Her thoughts drifted to the brief moment when her breath was all but stolen from her—the intensity of the officer's gaze and the undeniable chemistry that crackled between them. Could there be more to their connection than mere coincidence? Lexi couldn't help but entertain the possibility, her pulse quickening at the thought.

"Focus, Lexi," she scolded herself, though a part of her clung to the burgeoning hope in her chest.

⚜ ⚜ ⚜ ⚜

The following days were a blur as Lexi barked orders to the staff. Her mind was a whirl as she juggled all of the balls of the campaign. The lack of sleep was taking its toll, and she knew it. The late nights, bad diet, and worrying about her mom's cancer diagnosis weighed on her. All she wanted to do right now was pull the covers over her head and sleep for a week.

"Hey, Lexi, do you ever sleep?" Steve, a fellow campaign staffer, asked as he approached her desk.

"Sleep is overrated when there's an election to win," Lexi replied with a grin. "Besides, isn't that what coffee is for?"

"Speaking of which," Steve said, handing her a steaming cup. "I figured you could use this."

"Thanks, Steve. You're a lifesaver." She took a grateful sip. As the caffeine hit her system, Lexi refocused on the task at hand. There would be time for sleep later. Right now, there was an election to win and a world to change.

She couldn't shake the feeling that this campaign was more than just another job. It was a chance to prove herself and make a lasting impact on the political landscape. And she wouldn't rest until Congresswoman Marsh secured another term in office, because for Lexi, passion and commitment were everything.

After poring over the latest polling data, Lexi stood up and stretched, flexing as she reached for the sky and shook out her cramped legs. She glanced at the clock on the wall and let out an exasperated sigh.

"Is it seriously only three p.m.?" she muttered to herself, adjusting her polka-dot blouse before returning to analyze the campaign statistics.

"Lexi, I've got a new strategy idea," Steve called from across the office. "You're gonna love it."

"Alright, shoot," Lexi replied, leaning against her desk with crossed arms, her eyebrows raised in anticipation.

Steve grinned. "What if we organize a flash mob to support Congresswoman Marsh? It'll go viral!"

Lexi smirked and shook her head. "A flash mob? Really, Steve? This isn't 2018. We need something fresh and innovative." She paused for a moment, her mind racing with ideas. "What if we set up a series of impromptu town hall meetings, live-streamed on social media? Maybe set up a tiki-toki account, or whatever that social is. That way, we can showcase the congresswoman's accessibility and create real-time engagement."

"I guess you're right." Steve looked dejected at the suggestion. Did she need to embrace her Gen Z workers and look at their ideas? Maybe, but time was ticking and what she didn't want was the congresswoman looking like she was pandering to any particular generation. Besides, her numbers were good across the board.

"Flattery will get you everywhere, Steve," Lexi teased. But deep down, she was disappointed in herself, as it was her job to think on her feet and come up with creative solutions. After all, she graduated with a degree in political science from a prestigious university, and her quick wit and sharp intellect had always given her an edge.

"By the way," Steve said, lowering his voice conspiratorially, "I heard you were quite the troublemaker back in college. Any truth to those rumors?"

"Who, me?" Lexi feigned innocence, her green eyes twinkling with mischief. "I have no idea what you're talking about."

"Come on, Lexi," Steve prodded playfully. "I heard you once organized a massive protest against the administration's decision to cut funding for student clubs."

"Alright, fine," Lexi admitted, grinning sheepishly. "But it was for a good cause. And we got the funding reinstated, so I'd say it was worth the trouble."

"You've always been a force to be reckoned with," Steve said, his admiration for Lexi evident in his voice.

"Thanks, Steve. But it's not just about making a scene or stirring up controversy," Lexi explained, her expression softening as she reflected on her past experiences and the motivations that drove her. "It's about standing up for what's right and making a positive impact on the world. That's why I'm here, working tirelessly to help Congresswoman Marsh win this election."

She scanned the notes before her as her mind kicked into high gear. "Alright, let's brainstorm. Think about what topics our opponents might want to exploit and how we can counter them effectively."

As they huddled together, Lexi felt a familiar surge of excitement course through her.

"Great work today, everyone," Lexi announced later that evening as the staff began packing up their belongings. "We've got the big rally coming up this weekend, so let's hit the ground running tomorrow. We've got this!"

Lexi watched her colleagues leave as the campaign office darkened with the lack of movement, then rose from her chair, ready for a hot bath, a glass of wine, and her trashy romance novel. Slinging her purse across her body, she pulled out her keys, flipped the lights in her office off, and sighed.

"Another day in the grind," she said, walking to her car.

❦❦❦❦

Max stood tall and resolute next to her patrol car, her eyes scanning the horizon with a practiced ease, ever watchful for any sign of trouble. She adjusted her uniform cap, pulling it down slightly to shield her eyes from the glaring sun as it dipped below the horizon.

"Evening, Max," came a familiar voice over her walkie-talkie. Max smiled at the sound.

"Evening, dispatch," Max responded, her voice low and steady. "Quiet out here so far."

"Same here," the dispatcher replied, the faint crackle of static punctuating her words. "Let's hope it stays that way."

"Agreed." Max replaced the walkie-talkie on her shoulder, her fingers brushing against the cold metal of her nameplate as she did so.

She knew better than to let herself be lulled into a false sense of security, though. In her line of work, danger could strike without warning. Max's background as a former army soldier had taught her the value of vigilance, and she applied that lesson to her work as a highway patrol officer with unwavering commitment.

As Max continued her watch, her thoughts drifted momentarily to her colleagues at the station. They often joked about her no-nonsense demeanor and strict adherence to protocol, but beneath the teasing she hoped lay a deep respect for her abilities and dedication to the job.

Her thoughts were interrupted by the sudden crackle of her walkie-talkie. "Max, we've got a call for assistance on Route 8. Possible vehicle accident."

"Copy that," Max replied, her voice instantly back to its professional timbre as she climbed into the cruiser and started the engine. "On my way."

While some saw her strict adherence to rules as rigid, Max valued discipline and order. She followed protocol to the letter, never compromising her principles. Her stern demeanor could be off-putting to those who didn't know her well.

But underneath Max's tough exterior lay a wry sense of humor. She enjoyed exchanging good-natured banter with colleagues between calls. And she took immense satisfaction in apprehending criminals through clever maneuvers. Outsmarting lawbreakers gave her a thrill.

Max slowed the patrol car as she approached flashing hazard lights up ahead. She scanned the scene, noting details. A late-model sedan with a flat tire. An elderly man and woman standing outside the car looking upset and waving as she neared. No other vehicles stopped.

Max pulled up behind the disabled car and stepped out, one hand resting casually on her holstered gun.

"Afternoon, folks. What seems to be the trouble here?" she asked in an authoritative but friendly tone.

The elderly man gestured helplessly at the flat tire. "We got a blowout and don't have any money for a tow!" He had a slight quiver in his voice.

His wife wrung her hands anxiously. "And neither of us knows how to change a tire properly. We've never had this happen before!"

Max nodded reassuringly. "Not to worry, I can change that tire and get you folks on your way."

It was against the rules to change a tire for someone, but she just couldn't see how this old couple was going to be able to get some help. She opened their trunk to retrieve the necessary equipment, sizing up the situation. A basic tire change, no problem.

"You folks just relax in your car while I take care of this," Max instructed.

The elderly couple looked immensely relieved. "Bless you, Officer!" the woman said.

Max swiftly and efficiently swapped out the flat for the spare, her guard always up as she periodically scanned the surroundings. Satisfied there was no danger, she allowed herself a slight smile at the satisfaction of providing roadside assistance.

With the new tire installed and properly torqued, Max loaded the flat into their trunk to be repaired.

"There you go, good as new," Max said, giving the sedan a friendly pat. "Don't wait to get that flat fixed. Okay?"

"Thank you, Officer. There is a special place in heaven for people like you."

Max smiled, "I'm just doing my job, sir. Now you folks be careful. Have a good night."

The elderly man beamed as he and his wife profusely thanked Max. As they cautiously merged back onto the highway, Max waved, then headed back to her vehicle.

Settling into the driver's seat, Max decided to swing by the diner before returning to her route. She was craving one of their chocolate milkshakes, her secret vice.

The bell jingled as Max entered the cozy diner. She nodded to the familiar waitress before sliding into her regular booth.

"Let me guess...chocolate shake?" the waitress, Betty, asked with a knowing smile.

"You got me." Max laughed. "I'm predictable."

"Nah, just a woman who knows what she likes."

Max smiled, appreciating the banter. She might be uptight on duty, but she enjoyed loosening up a bit on her own time.

Sipping the thick milkshake, Max gazed out the window into the darkness, feeling content. She loved the order and discipline of her job but welcomed these small indulgences too. It was all about balance, something drilled into her as a soldier.

Duty always called, but for now, she would savor this brief rest.

Max sighed as she finished up her milkshake. Standing, she dropped cash on the table for Betty.

꙳꙳꙳꙳

Officer Church recognized the Lexus the moment it entered the highway. Not because it did something to warrant closer inspection, but because she was familiar with the license plate—and the knock-down gorgeous brunette she'd stopped once already. She couldn't help but notice the vehicle's speed though for a couple of miles.

As she followed behind the Lexus, Officer Church debated whether or not to pull her over. While she understood the importance of following the rules, she also didn't want to make life difficult for Lexi Anders, someone who was simply doing her own job, albeit at head-scratching speeds.

"Better safe than sorry," she decided finally, flipping her lights and reaching for her radio to call in the stop.

꙳꙳꙳꙳

As Lexi glanced in the mirror once more, her heart sank at the sight of flashing red and blues. She couldn't help but wonder what this encounter would bring, not just for herself, but for everyone involved in Congresswoman Marsh's campaign.

The flashing lights in her rearview mirror were like a physical blow to Lexi's chest, the air whooshing out of her lungs as she reluctantly eased off the gas pedal and guided her car to the side of the road. Her hands trembled on the steering wheel, and she clenched her jaw tightly, attempting to regain some semblance of control. She knew she had to focus, but panic was beginning to cloud her thoughts.

"Get it together, Lexi," she muttered under her breath as the patrol car pulled up behind her, the red and blue glare illuminating the interior of her vehicle. The officer stepped from the cruiser, the tall, athletic figure silhouetted against the burning light of the spotlight practically blinding her. Even at a distance, Lexi could recognize the determination that radiated from the officer as she approached.

"Good evening, ma'am," Officer Church said, her voice firm and steady. "You're starting to make this a habit."

Lexi sighed. "Not again."

"I'm afraid so. License, please. You do have your license this time, right?"

"Of course. Third time's a charm." Lexi pulled it out from her purse and handed it to Office Church.

"Excuse me?"

"Nothing, just mumbling to myself. Was I driving too slow again?"

"Not this time. You were actually speeding." Officer Church took her documents and looked them over. "Going home?"

"As a matter of fact, I was."

"Is this your correct address?"

"It is."

"Okay, give me a minute." Officer Church walked back to her cruiser.

Lexi watched the swagger of Officer Church as she walked back to her car. There was something sexy about a woman in uniform. It wasn't lost on Lexi that the power the officer exuded was a tad intoxicating.

Within minutes she was back at Lexi's window. She handed back her license and registration. "I'm afraid I'm going to have to give you a ticket this time."

"Seriously?"

"I'm afraid so."

"Fine," Lexi said, tossing her documents on the front seat. She grabbed the ticket box, scribbled her signature, and handed it back.

"Have a nice evening, and please watch your speed. I would hate to have to meet you like this again." She smiled, handing Lexi the ticket.

Lexi rolled her window up as Officer Church walked back to her cruiser.

"Well, I wouldn't," she murmured. There was something about the officer that made Lexi want to know—no, need to know—more about her. Maybe there was a way she could get a little closer without it looking like she was trying to get a little revenge for the ticket. Besides, Congresswoman Marsh's campaign had an opening on her security detail, and as they got closer to the election, she'd garnered her share of threats around her policies on gentrification and other progressive social issues. So, it was perfect timing. Besides, if something popped in the officer's background check, she could bail on the idea easily enough.

She knew a guy who could dig up information on just about anyone. If there were any skeletons lurking in Officer Church's closet, he'd find them. She tapped at her phone and dialed a number.

"Hey, it's Lexi," she said, her voice steady and confident. "I need some background info on someone. Think you can help me out?"

"Sure thing, Lexi," came the reply from the other end. "Just send me the details, and I'll see what I can do."

"Thanks," she replied, giving Officer Church's name and her position. Hanging up, her heart pounded with a mix of anticipation and anxiety as she considered the possible outcomes.

"No good deed goes unpunished," she reminded herself, taking a deep breath.

Chapter Seven

The heavy oak door shut behind them with a soft, decisive click. Congresswoman Marsh and Lexi stood in the dimly lit private office, its walls lined with shelves of leather-bound books and framed photographs. The air was thick with tension, as if the very room held its breath.

"Please, sit down," Marsh said, her voice wavering slightly. She gestured to the two high-backed chairs on either side of her polished mahogany desk. Lexi took a seat, her eyes never leaving the congresswoman's face. There was a vulnerability in the older woman's expression that Lexi hadn't seen before, a crack in her usually unshakable facade.

"Lexi," Marsh began, wringing her hands together in her lap. "There's something I need to tell you. Something that could threaten my entire campaign."

"Congresswoman, whatever it is, we can handle it," Lexi replied, trying to project confidence even as her heart raced with concern.

Taking a deep breath, Marsh looked Lexi straight in the eye. "I'm being blackmailed."

"Blackmailed?" Lexi echoed, her mind racing with questions and possible scenarios. "By whom? What do they want?"

"Someone who knows about…about the situation involving Will and his girlfriend," she confessed, her eyes welling up with tears. "They have information that could destroy not only my career, but William's life as well. He did something at university that I had to…let's just say…take care of."

"We need to contact the FBI."

"No, no I can't expose Will's life to the media. That's a last resort. Besides, this just might be a hoax. We get them all the time."

"Congresswoman, I'll do everything in my power to protect you and your son, but this seems more than a hoax," Lexi said, the urgency of the situation settling heavily in her chest.

Marsh nodded, her gaze fixed on the floor. "I want to wait. We have a good security team in place, and I trust them to do their jobs." She paused, swallowing hard.

"Congresswoman, we'll find a way to resolve this. We'll get through it, but I still think we need to contact the FBI," Lexi said.

"I know, but for now I'm vetoing that idea. Thank you, Lexi. I just don't know how much more of this I can take," Marsh admitted, her voice wavering. She looked up at Lexi, the vulnerability in her eyes deepening. "If this information gets out, it could ruin everything."

"Let's take it one step at a time," Lexi suggested, her tone gentle but firm. "We need to gather all the facts and figure out who we're dealing with. I will do everything in my power to protect you, your family, and this campaign."

Marsh sighed, tears brimming in her eyes. "I wish I could be as strong as you are, Lexi."

"Strength isn't about never being afraid or vulnerable, Congresswoman," Lexi replied softly. "It's about facing our fears and moving forward despite them." She reached across the desk, placing her hand on top of Marsh's. "You've got this far, and you have an entire team behind you. We all believe in you."

Tears rolled down Marsh's cheek as she squeezed Lexi's hand. "Thank you, Lexi. Your unwavering support means the world to me."

"Of course, Congresswoman," Lexi reassured her. "Now, let's get down to business. Do you have any idea who might be behind the blackmail or what they want from you?"

"Other than their demands for me to resign my campaign, I'm not sure." Marsh wiped away tears with her free hand. "They seem to know every detail of Will's life, including his relationship with Jenny."

"Then that's where we'll start." Lexi's mind was already racing with plans and strategies. "We'll dig into Will's life and connections, as well as any leads on who could be behind this."

"Alright," Marsh said, her voice steadier now. "But Lexi, please…be careful. I don't want this leaking to the press."

"Congresswoman, your problems are my problems," Lexi said, then took a breath before voicing her next idea. "I think we should bring in someone with a unique skill set to help us navigate this situation," Lexi said, her voice filled with conviction and determination. "I think I know someone who could be valuable in helping us uncover the truth behind this blackmail plot."

"Who are you thinking of?" Marsh asked, her brow furrowed in concern.

"An Officer Church," Lexi replied, watching Congresswoman Marsh's expression closely. "She's a former army soldier and has extensive counterterrorism and tactical experience. Plus, she's worked on high-stakes investigations before."

"Should I ask how you know this woman?" Marsh gave Lexi a   suspicious look.

"Honestly, she's—"

Marsh raised her hand. "Please don't tell me you two are in a relationship/."

"What? No, of course not. I don't have that kind of time for a relationship."

"Good."

"She's pulled me over twice recently…"

The congresswoman palmed her forehead.

"It's okay. She only gave me one ticket. She was very discreet and frankly, I was impressed with how she handled herself. So, I had a friend check her out and she's got a very impressive background. I think she would be perfect and she can easily blend in. I think we should consider adding her to the team."

Marsh hesitated, clearly weighing the pros and cons of involving someone else in their predicament. "I'm not sure, Lexi. How can we be certain that she won't have any conflicts of interest, given her position?"

"I understand your concerns," Lexi said, her eyes locked onto Marsh's. "But sometimes, we need to take calculated risks to achieve success. And right now, we need all the help we can get. Trusting Officer Church could get access to areas that might be the key to saving your campaign and protecting Will."

Congresswoman Marsh stood by the expansive window, her gaze fixed on the city skyline, seemingly lost in thought. In the dimly lit room, the darkness outside seemed to be creeping in, mirroring the heavy atmosphere that hung over them. Lexi watched her carefully, noting the subtle tremble in the congresswoman's hands as she clutched at the blackmail letter.

"Alright, Lexi," Marsh conceded after a moment of contemplation. "If you believe that Officer Church is the right person to help us, then I trust your judgment. But please, be absolutely certain that she's on our side."

"Thank you, Congresswoman," Lexi replied, her voice filled with gratitude and determination. "I promise you, Max will be an invaluable ally in this fight. Together, we'll get to the bottom of this blackmail plot and make sure your campaign emerges stronger than ever."

The air in the room seemed to shift, as if a weight had been lifted from both of their shoulders. Though the road ahead would undoubtedly be fraught with challenges, but at least now Lexi had another ally to help her navigate a terrain that had the potential to derail a fantastic political career.

"I'll get her commander's information, but I think the request to have her put on your team would be better coming from you."

Marsh looked over at her and nodded. Lexi could see the pain in her eyes. Hopefully, Officer Church could help them get to the bottom of the blackmail scheme. Now, the biggest hurdle Lexi faced was explaining to the officer exactly how she had gotten onto the congresswoman's radar. That might prove to be a little more difficult to navigate.

༄༄༄༄

The rhythmic tap of Lexi's heels echoed through the marble-floored hallway as she made her way toward the campaign staff meeting room a few days later. As she rounded the corner, she caught sight of Sarah and Ethan engaged in lively conversation, their voices a blend of laughter and professionalism.

"Alright everyone, let's get started," Congresswoman Marsh announced, her tone authoritative but warm. The group took their seats around the large table, its glossy surface reflecting the soft light from the chandelier above.

"Before we dive into our updates, I just want to express how proud I am of the diverse and talented team we've assembled here," Marsh said, smiling at each staff member. "Our diversity is not only essential for representing the constituents we serve, but it also strengthens our ideas and strategies."

A murmur of agreement rippled through the room. Lexi felt a surge of pride in the congresswoman's words, knowing that the addition of Officer Church would only further enhance that diversity. As the meeting progressed, Lexi found herself stealing glances at the empty chair beside her, imagining Max's strong presence and the impact she could have on the campaign.

"Lexi?" Congresswoman Marsh's voice brought Lexi back to the present, her eyes meeting the congresswoman's questioning gaze.

"Sorry, Congresswoman. Just lost in thought for a moment," Lexi admitted, trying to suppress her eagerness. The butterflies that fluttered in her stomach made her smile inward. She knew she needed to maintain her professionalism, but there was something about Max, a magnetic pull that was hard to ignore.

"Keep it together, Lexi," she scolded herself silently as she collected her belongings at the close of the meeting. With a deep breath, Lexi turned her attention back to the tasks at hand, determined to excel in her role while keeping her personal feelings in check.

After a few hours of focused work, Lexi stepped outside for a moment of respite, determined to enjoy the beautiful sunset that was casting long shadows on the campaign headquarters as the throngs of people below had reduced to barely a stream of pedestrians. She leaned against the brick wall, feeling its rough texture beneath her fingertips, grounding her to the present.

"Lexi!" Sarah called out, striding quickly toward her. "Congresswoman Marsh wants you in the strategy meeting."

"Right." Lexi exhaled slowly, pushing off from the wall. So much for going home early. Her work-life balance sucked, but she knew it wouldn't last forever. Hopefully. Her mother was going to need her more than ever now, and she needed to make sure she was as available—or at least as available as possible with the demands of this campaign. Her weekly phone calls to her mom had become daily. Cynthia kept reassuring her that she was fine, but Lexi wasn't convinced. If Lexi was struggling with the diagnosis, her mom had to be going through hell, not to mention what would happen once her father found out. Keeping secrets from someone you loved was ultimately toxic, no matter the intention.

She sighed as she walked to the meeting. She wanted to tell the congresswoman about her mom, but she didn't want her family's business out there, especially since she hadn't cleared it with Cynthia. Besides, the congresswoman had her own problems to deal with at the moment.

Inside the conference room, Lexi listened intently to the discussion on voter outreach, occasionally interjecting with her own insights. But as the conversation ebbed, her thoughts drifted out of the office and somewhere else that found her getting to know a certain compelling highway patrol officer on a much more intimate basis.

"Lexi?" Ethan asked, waving a hand in front of her face. "You with us?"

"Sorry," she replied, shaking her head. "Just lost in thought for a moment."

"Understandable," he said with a knowing smile. "It's been a long day."

As the meeting wound down, Lexi hung back as the congresswoman chatted with a few staffers. Marsh noticed her waiting and dismissed the others, shuffling her notes into a neat pile until the two were alone.

"Congresswoman," Lexi began cautiously. "I think it would be a good idea for me to spend some time with Officer Church once she joins our team. It'll help me get a sense of her skills and capabilities before we fully integrate her into our security detail."

"Good idea," March agreed. "We want to ensure a smooth transition. I've spoken to Officer Church's commander, and he's willing to loan her to us. On a temporary basis."

"Temporary? Well I...I just thought we could—"

"Lexi, it's the best we can do right now. I had to squeeze to get him to agree to loan her to us at all. So, let's make the best of it, shall we?"

"Yes, Congresswoman."

As Lexi walked away, she couldn't help but feel a sense of anticipation for what lay ahead. The possibility of working closely with Officer Church held a thrilling allure that she couldn't ignore.

Chapter Eight

"Officer Church, I have news for you," Captain Jones said, his eyes serious as they met Max's gaze.

Max straightened her back, sensing that whatever was about to come wasn't going to be good. She had been working hard in the Highway Patrol, earning a reputation for being determined and honorable. She was a valuable asset to the force and she knew it, but Jones's tone didn't sound like she was being promoted or given another commendation.

"Sir?" she asked, her eyes narrowing with suspicion.

"You're being reassigned, effective immediately," he replied, handing her an official-looking envelope.

"Reassigned? To where?" Max asked, her voice rising with concern. She tore open the envelope and scanned the contents within. Her heart sank as she read the words on the page: she was to head the security detail for Congresswoman Marsh's campaign.

"Congresswoman Marsh? Why?" Max couldn't help but feel slighted by the sudden change in her career trajectory. She had devoted her life to law enforcement, not politics.

"Orders from higher up. You know how it goes, Church. It's out of my hands." Jones offered her a sympathetic look, but it did little to quell the anger bubbling inside her.

"Is this some kind of joke?" Max blurted out.

Even her hair seemed to bristle with indignation. "Captain, I've put in years of service, risked my life countless times, and now I'm being reduced to a glorified bodyguard?"

"Max." Jones lowered his voice, trying to keep her calm. "This isn't a demotion. Congresswoman Marsh is a high-profile target, and she specifically requested someone with your skills and experience."

"Specifically requested? I don't even know her!" Max retorted, her anger getting the better of her. In her mind, she couldn't help but wonder if someone had it out for her. Was this some kind of punishment, or a way to get her off the force?

"Well, she knows you." Jones sighed, running a hand through his hair. "Look, I know you're frustrated, but think about it. This could be a great opportunity for you. You'll still be serving your country, just in a different capacity."

"Sir, with all due respect, I didn't sign up for politics," Max said through gritted teeth. Her mind raced with thoughts about who could have orchestrated such a change, and why.

"Sometimes we don't get to choose how we serve, Officer Church. It's part of the job," Jones replied sternly.

Max clenched her fists at her sides, trying to contain her disappointment and anger. She knew he was right, but that didn't make the news any easier to swallow. As she looked down at the reassignment papers in her hands, she couldn't shake the feeling that something more was at play here—and she intended to find out what that something was.

☙ ☙ ❧ ❧

Max stood on the sidewalk, staring at the imposing glass building that housed Congresswoman Marsh's campaign headquarters. The sun glinted off the windows casting a harsh, almost blinding light onto the street below. She took a deep breath, her hand gripping the strap of her duffel bag with determination. Her journey to this place had been a quiet one, filled with conflicting emotions and unanswered questions.

"Here goes nothing," she muttered under her breath, her heart pounding in anticipation of uncertain territory.

As Max stepped through the sliding glass doors, the cool air-conditioning hit her like a shockwave, chasing away the heat of the day and sending a shiver down her spine. She couldn't help but feel like she was walking into the lion's den. The bustling atmosphere inside the campaign headquarters only served to heighten her nerves. A throng of volunteers hustled back and forth, faces flushed with excitement and purpose. Phones rang incessantly, the cacophony punctuated by murmured conversations and the rapid-fire tapping of keyboards. She immediately noticed the lack of security protocols at the front door and didn't see any security personnel walking the floor.

"Officer Church?" a voice called out, snapping her out of her thoughts.

She turned to see a petite woman approaching with a tight smile plastered on her face. Max noticed how the woman's eyes flickered over her uniform, taking in every detail. She felt exposed and vulnerable, something she wasn't used to.

"Welcome to the nerve center of Congresswoman

Marsh's campaign. I'm Sarah, the press secretary," she said, her voice strained as if she were trying too hard to be friendly. "I'll take you to meet the team."

"Thank you," Max replied tersely, her mind racing with thoughts of Lexi Anders. Was it possible that the spunky, intelligent woman she'd met during those chance encounters was somehow responsible for her sudden reassignment? And if so, why? She couldn't shake the nagging feeling that there was more to this story than she knew.

"Right this way," Sarah said, leading Max down a long hallway lined with posters of Congresswoman Marsh. The congresswoman's face smiled back at her from every angle, a constant reminder of the political world she was now immersed in.

Max's heart hammered in her chest as they rounded a corner and entered a large, open-concept office space. The atmosphere was tense, charged with the energy of people working tirelessly toward a common goal. She could feel their eyes on her as she followed Sarah through the room, and Max suddenly felt like the new kid coming into class halfway through the semester.

"Everyone," Sarah announced, raising her voice just enough to be heard above the din. "I'd like to introduce Officer Maxine Church, our new head of security."

A murmur rippled through the crowd, and Max felt the stress of their scrutiny bearing down on her. She squared her shoulders, meeting their gazes with a steely resolve, determined not to let them see how much this situation unnerved her.

"Nice to meet you all," Max muttered, forcing a tight smile onto her lips. Despite her best efforts to maintain her composure, her eyes scanned the room for one person in particular—the elusive Lexi Anders. She did not immediately locate her.

"Officer Church, it's an honor to have you on our team," Congresswoman Marsh said warmly, extending her hand. "I've heard great things about your service to our nation, and I believe you'll be a tremendous asset to us." She leaned in closer and said conspiratorially, "I think you can lose the uniform, Officer Church. Business casual will be just fine. I don't want the troops thinking they're under investigation or something."

"Yes, ma'am. Thank you, Congresswoman," Max replied, shaking the congresswoman's hand firmly. She felt a spark of pride at the recognition, but it was overshadowed by her frustration with the situation. "Please call me Max."

"Let me introduce you to everyone," Congresswoman Marsh continued, gesturing around the room. "You've already met Sarah, our press secretary. This is Ethan, my chief of staff. Hank and Jules, who will be working with you in security. And my son, Will."

Recognition flashed when she looked at Hank. "Seventy-fifth Ranger regiment. Am I right?"

"Yes, ma'am. Second battalion."

"At ease, Hank. We're just civilians," she whispered, hoping no one noticed Hank snapping to.

Hank relaxed a little, but he definitely carried himself with all the pride of an Army Ranger. She smiled down at Jules, also vaguely familiar, and wondered where she knew her from. It wasn't coming to her, but she'd remember. She never forgot a face. A name, yep, but a face, no.

"Nice to meet you all," Max said again, but then

her gaze found the face she had been searching for.

After the two traffic stops and the search of her... toy bag...Max had made up several stories about Lexi Anders to assuage her curiosity, with varying degrees of intrigue, fantasy, and—though she wasn't proud of it—lust. But once she'd been reassigned and determined that Lexi was behind this new position, those thoughts changed to cast her as an irritating nuisance who was set on messing with Max's life. Once that got into her head, it was easy to see that Lexi was using her power to get back at her for the speeding ticket. Typical politics, dirty and petty. So disappointing.

But she hadn't expected Lexi to be so...ordinary in her everyday life. Standing before her now, average height, brown hair, brown eyes—Max saw nothing that screamed master manipulator. That, perhaps, was the most disappointing of all.

"Lexi?" Congresswoman Marsh prompted, noticing Max's attention. "This is Alexandra Anders, my campaign manager. She's been indispensable to my success so far."

"Nice to meet you, Officer Church," Lexi said smoothly, a hint of challenge in her eyes as she extended her hand.

"I believe we've already met, Ms. Anders," Max replied icily, struggling to keep her voice neutral as she took Lexi's hand. She had no doubt now that Lexi was the reason for her new duty assignment. The contact sent a jolt of electricity through her, making her realize just how much she had underestimated Lexi in almost every aspect.

"Alright, everyone," Congresswoman Marsh called out, clapping her hands together. "Let's give Officer Church some space to settle in. We have a lot of work to do!"

Marsh turned to Max and extended her hand again, but her voice held an edge that wasn't there before. "It's great to have you on the team. If you don't mind, when you get settled, can I see you in my office? As soon as possible."

"Of course," Max said.

"Great, let's get back to work, everyone."

Max watched Marsh's retreating back. Her shoulders slumped, her eyes seemed to brim with sadness, and something about sudden mood change confused Max.

As the team dispersed, Max turned to Lexi, her mind racing. It was obvious now that Lexi had orchestrated her reassignment. She had likely been the one to recommend Max for the job, aware of her military background and spotless record. But why? Was all of this really just payback for the speeding ticket? It seemed extreme.

"Is there something on your mind, Officer Church?" Lexi asked, her eyes narrowing as she observed Max's expression.

"Actually, yes," Max replied, her jaw set. "I can't help but wonder why I'm here." She paused, watching Lexi's reaction carefully. "It seems like quite the coincidence that I get reassigned to work for you just after our..." She hesitated, searching for the right word. "Interaction."

Lexi's expression remained carefully neutral, but Max could see a flicker of amusement in her eyes. "Well, Officer Church, sometimes life is full of coincidences," she said smoothly before turning on her heel and walking away, leaving Max standing there with more questions than answers.

Max's heart pounded in her chest as she watched Lexi walk away. She knew Lexi was responsible for her reassignment, but she didn't understand why. And even more confusing were the feelings that Lexi stirred within her, strong feelings of attraction she hadn't felt in a very long time. She had no intention of acting on those particular feelings, so she went with what was the most comfortable one—anger.

"Ms. Anders," Max called out. Lexi stopped in her tracks and slowly turned to face Max, a knowing smile playing at the corners of her mouth.

"Officer Church," she replied coolly, crossing her arms over her chest. "What can I do for you?"

Max's nostrils flared as she closed the distance between them, stopping just inches from Lexi's face. The air crackled with tension, and around them, staff members unconvincingly pretended not to notice the brewing confrontation. "You know damn well what this is about," Max hissed through gritted teeth.

"Enlighten me." Lexi's voice was steady, but Max could see the hint of defiance flickering in her eyes.

"Cut the crap, Ms. Anders," she snapped, trying to maintain some semblance of control. "I know you're the reason I've been reassigned. You pulled strings to get me here."

"Did I?" Lexi raised an eyebrow, feigning innocence. "And what exactly would be my motive for that, Officer Church?"

"I don't know which was more humiliating, the speeding ticket or the sex toys, but either could have made you want to seek revenge. Maybe you wanted to keep an eye on me after our little run-in. Or maybe you just like having a loyal lapdog around." Max's words were laced with venom, but beneath her anger, there was a sliver of disappointment.

"Wow," Lexi drawled, her gaze never leaving Max's. "You really think I'm that manipulative, huh? That I'd go to such lengths just to...what? Keep you close?"

"Prove me wrong," Max challenged, her jaw clenched so tightly it ached.

"Believe whatever you want, Officer Church," Lexi said with a shrug, her expression cold and unreadable. "But if you're going to work here, I suggest you focus on your job, not on baseless accusations."

Max's chest burned with fury, but she knew Lexi was right. She couldn't let her personal feelings— her anger, confusion, and the undeniable attraction that still lingered between them—interfere with her responsibilities. She was here to protect Congresswoman Marsh and her campaign, not to engage in petty arguments with Lexi Anders.

"Fine," Max muttered, forcing herself to take a step back from Lexi. "But just so we're clear. I'm *not* your lapdog. I'm here to do a job, and that's it."

"Officer Church, I don't know what you want me to say." Lexi sighed, her eyes flicking away from Max's unyielding gaze. "So, I'll just hold my tongue."

"Try the truth for once," Max snapped, frustration boiling in her gut as she crossed her arms defensively over her chest. "Did you have anything to do with my reassignment? Yes or no?"

"Officer Church, I told you before—" Lexi began, but Max cut her off, her voice rising in anger.

"Damn it, Ms. Anders! Just answer the question." She clenched her fists at her sides, fighting to keep her emotions in check. This conversation was only making it more difficult to maintain the professional distance she had vowed to uphold.

Lexi crossed her arms, and Max recognized the defensive posture that almost always meant the suspect was lying. Her voice was tight. "No, I didn't have anything to do with it."

"Then why am I here?" Max asked, her voice barely a whisper as she struggled to keep her composure.

"Officer Church," Lexi began hesitantly, reaching out a hand as if to bridge the gap that had formed between them. "I know you're upset—"

"Save it, Ms. Anders," Max interrupted, stepping back to avoid her touch.

"Fine," Lexi said quietly as she turned away. "Let's get to work then."

"I need to meet the security team and see what protocols have been set," Max said curtly to Lexi's back.

"Of course," Lexi replied without turning around.

⁂

"Max, can I see you in the congresswoman's office?" Lexi poked her head through the door.

Max looked up from the week's events laid out on the desk and nodded. She stretched her neck as she stood and followed Lexi into the office. "I'll be back," she said to Ethan and Jules. "We can finalize the security details then."

Max watched the way Lexi's hip swayed and wondered… Damn, she needed to stop doing that and keep her mind focused.

"Please have a seat, Office Church." Marsh swept her hand toward the small leather couch across from her desk.

"Ma'am."

"How are you settling in? That's a stupid question, you just got here." Marsh rested her chin on her hands.

"This isn't my first rodeo, so I settle pretty quickly."

"Good, I'm sure you're getting the lay of the land."

"I am, ma'am."

Max looked at Lexi and then back to the congresswoman. The tension between them could be cut with a butter knife. Something wasn't quite right.

"Ma'am, why am I here?" Max leaned forward, sitting on the edge of the couch. Always be prepared, she told herself.

"Officer Church, what I am about to tell you can't leave this room."

Max noticed Lexi fidgeting. Her leg gently bounced, and she doubted Lexi even knew she was doing it. Max knew the way stress affected the nervous system and how it was mindlessly controlled. Her gaze landed on Marsh, who licked her lips and then dry-swallowed. Another nervous indicator.

"Ma'am, I'm sure whatever you're about to tell me isn't as bad as you think it is, so let's try and get through this. No judgment here." Deep down inside, Max was hoping Marsh was just going to tell her she'd made a mistake bringing her on board and she would be able to return to her job.

"You're right, I just need to take the bull by the horns and get this over with."

Here it comes, Max thought.

"I'm being blackmailed, and they are using an issue with   my son to get me to drop out of the race."

Whoa. That was not what Max was expecting. She felt herself being pulled to Lexi, who looked away as soon as Max looked at her. Her heart sank in dread and guilt. Now she felt like an asshole accusing Lexi of trying to get payback by having her assigned to the congresswoman's detail.

"So, this is why I'm really here?"

Marsh nodded, then looked over at Lexi and said, "I'm afraid so. Lexi says your background makes you the perfect person to help us."

Max sighed. Yep, she had egg all over her face as she remembered their encounter earlier.

"Okay," Max said, pulling a small note pad out of her breast pocket and clicking her pen. "Tell me why they think they can blackmail you to get out of the race."

Marsh walked around the desk, sat in a high-back leather chair next to the couch, and steepled her hands, looking at Max. "When Will was in college...he was arrested for dealing drugs, and a weapons charge."

Max's eyebrows shot up.

"The weapon was a knife that he carried every day, so it wasn't a gun, but they considered it a dangerous weapon in the commission of a felony." Marsh swallowed hard. "I used my influence to get the charges dismissed and buried. How Brown found out about it I have no idea, but now he's using it to blackmail me."

Max scribbled at the pertinent details and then asked, "How did he get the drugs?"

"He was using at the time, and before you ask, I didn't know. His buddy introduced him to his dealer. Which was convenient, because he got into some issues with money and his dealer suggested he start dealing for him at the university. Said it was a built-in clientele and Will could clear his debt and make a ton of money. So, he did."

"I see. How do you think Brown found out about this?"

"I have no idea."

"Does Will have a picture of this drug dealer?"

"Funny you should ask. Seems like the drug dealer liked palling around with a congresswoman's kid, so he stuck to Will like glue in the beginning."

"Did Will ID him to the police?"

The look on Marsh's face reminded Max of what she'd done.

"Sorry, sorry. Do you have photos?"

Marsh nodded as she got up and rounded her desk. Pulling a large envelope from the drawer, she handed it to Max and sighed.

Max pulled the photos out and spread them across the table. She studied each and every detail, from location, clothing, cars—anything that could help identify the dealer.

Lexi sat next to Max and took a few of the photos. "This looks familiar," Lexi said. "I remember it from my days when I visited the campus for political rallies."

"Really, how?" Max said, looking at the photo. "Did Will go to uni here?"

Marsh nodded.

"Well, that helps." Max stuffed the photos back into the envelope. "Can I keep these?"

"Of course."

"I have a friend from my military days who can help with this. Do you mind if I give him a call?"

"Can he be trusted?"

"Discretion is his middle name."

"I appreciate any help you can offer, Officer Church."

"We'll figure this out. Don't worry."

❧❧❧❧

Max stood at the window, watching the city lights flicker in the distance.

"Officer Church," a voice said softly behind her, making her startle. She turned to see Lexi standing there, concern etched on her face. "We need to go over some security protocols for tomorrow."

"Of course," Max replied, her voice steady despite the turmoil inside her. "Let's get started."

As they sat down, Max couldn't help but notice the way the fluorescent lights reflected off Lexi's hair, giving it an almost ethereal quality. The sight stirred something within her, a yearning she tried so desperately to suppress. But she knew that any hint of vulnerability could compromise her professional integrity, and she couldn't afford to let that happen.

"Congresswoman Marsh is scheduled to speak at two rallies tomorrow," Lexi began, her voice all business as she handed Max a detailed itinerary.

"Considering what I've just learned, I've arranged for additional security at both locations, but I think we should also discuss our response plan in case of any unforeseen incidents," Max said, keeping her distance from Lexi. She focused her attention on the document before her. As she scanned through the information, she took a deep breath to center herself, reminding herself she had a job to do. Congresswoman Marsh was depending on her to keep her safe, and Max would not let personal matters stand in the way of her duty.

"Do you have any specific concerns about these events?" Max asked, looking up from the papers.

"Nothing concrete," Lexi admitted. "But given

the current political climate, I think it's prudent to be prepared for anything."

"Understood." Max nodded, beginning to outline potential threats and the appropriate response measures. As she spoke, Lexi listened intently, occasionally chiming in with her own suggestions or concerns. Their conversation was fluid and efficient, a testament to their ability to work together despite the tension that simmered beneath the surface.

"Officer Church," Lexi said softly once they had finished discussing the security arrangements. "I know things between us are...complicated. But I want you to know I have nothing but respect for your professionalism and dedication to this job."

"Thank you, Ms. Anders," Max replied evenly, refusing to let herself be drawn into an emotional conversation. "I appreciate that."

"Of course."

"Is there anything else we need to discuss?" Max asked, hoping to bring the meeting to a close before her resolve crumbled.

"Actually, there is," Lexi said hesitantly, and Max steeled herself for whatever was coming next. "I've been thinking...I know we have our professional obligations, but I think it's important for both of us to acknowledge what's going on between us."

"Ms. Anders, I..." Max began, struggling to find the right words. "We have a job to do, and I suggest that you put whatever you think you are feeling aside for the good of the campaign."

"I understand. Are you holding a grudge?" Lexi asked softly, her voice tinged with hurt.

"Right now, I need to focus on Congresswoman Marsh and her safety. I don't have time to hold a grudge and frankly, it's not professional. So, whatever happened, or how it happened, is irrelevant. We just need to be able to maintain a professional relationship," Max replied firmly, hating herself for the pain she saw in Lexi's eyes but knowing she had no other choice.

"Alright," Lexi said quietly, her voice barely more than a whisper.

"Thank you," Max murmured.

As the evening wore on, Max maintained her distance from Lexi, acutely aware of the unresolved tension that lingered between them. Their conversations were strictly professional, their interactions polite but impersonal. Max knew she had made the right choice in prioritizing her duties over any potential conflict. She would focus on the job at hand and the safety of Congresswoman Marsh. That was her duty, and she would not let anything—or anyone—distract her from it. With each passing moment, Max felt the distance between her and Lexi growing.

Chapter Nine

L exi stepped into the elevator that took her to the bustling campaign headquarters, her heartbeat quickening. A mix of anticipation and nervousness churned in her stomach at the thought of seeing Max again after their tense exchange yesterday. Lexi swallowed hard, reminding herself that she was here to work on Congresswoman Marsh's campaign, not to dwell on personal matters.

"Morning, Lexi!" Sarah called out as she rushed past, a stack of papers in her hands.

"Hey, Sarah," Lexi replied, forcing a smile onto her face. She glanced around, searching for any sign of Max among the sea of faces. She couldn't help herself despite their rocky interactions so far—or, perhaps, because of them.

Her gaze finally landed on the tall, athletic figure of Max as she conversed with Hank and Jules from the security team. Max had lost the patrol uniform and exchanged it for a smart-looking button-down with a blazer that looked like it was custom made, dress slacks, and polished lace-up boots. Odd footwear, Lexi thought, but she took a moment to appreciate the way the sunlight caught Max's short, dirty blond hair, casting a golden halo around her head.

Oh, that is so...appropriate for someone like Max. An angel.

"Keep it together, Lexi," she muttered under her breath, trying to stave off her growing infatuation.

She had a job to do, and so did Max. But Lexi couldn't shake the feeling that there was more to Max than met the eye, and while she respected what Max had said last night, there was something in her determined to break down the wall between them, even just a little.

"Hey, Ethan," Lexi said as she approached the chief of staff, who was busy sucking on his vape pen while scribbling notes on a whiteboard. "Do you know if I'll be working with Officer Church on anything today?"

"Umm…" Ethan paused, scanning the list of tasks for the day. "Yeah, looks like you two are assigned to coordinate security measures for the upcoming event with all those government bigwigs."

"Okay, great," Lexi replied, a determined glint in her eye. She wasn't about to let Max deter her from doing her job. This was an opportunity she couldn't afford to waste.

"Good luck with that one," Ethan said as he exhaled a cloud of vapor. "Church seems like she is one tough cookie."

"Yes, she does. Duty first," Lexi replied, her heart pounding in her ears.

❧ ❧ ❧ ❧

Lexi stood at the edge of the room, her gaze locked on Officer Church. Max's jaw was set in a rigid line, her steely cold stare distant as she scanned the room, looking like a sheepdog guarding its flock of lambs. She was every bit the formidable highway patrol officer, her athletic frame accentuating the sense of authority she commanded. It was clear that Max wasn't thrilled to be working alongside Lexi and the team, but the tension only fueled Lexi's determination to break through the icy exterior.

"Excuse me," Lexi said, approaching Max with a warm smile. "I just wanted to make sure we're on the same page for the upcoming event."

"Of course," Max replied curtly, her eyes never leaving the tablet in her hands. Her voice held an unmistakable chill.

"Great," Lexi continued, doing her best to ignore the sting of rejection. "I thought we could start by going over the guest list and identifying any potential security risks."

"Okay," Max muttered, finally raising her eyes to meet Lexi's. For a moment, Lexi felt a flicker of hope, only to watch it extinguish in the frosty depths of Max's stare.

Lexi couldn't help but steal glances at Max as Max explained the details for the event. She noticed the way Max's fingers danced over the tablet, the slight furrow of her brow when she concentrated. Each subtle detail sent a shiver down Lexi's spine, her heart racing with the realization that her feelings for Max were growing stronger. She tried to refocus on the task at hand, but her thoughts kept drifting back to Max, the unspoken electricity between them crackling like a live wire, or maybe that was just her.

"Here," Max said, handing Lexi a document without looking up from her work. As their fingers brushed together, Lexi felt a spark of warmth amid the iciness. She held on to the sensation. Lexi liked a challenge, and Max was starting to become just that.

"Thanks," Lexi whispered, her voice barely audible. She continued to work in silence, her mind racing with conflicting emotions. Was this just an ill-advised crush, or something more? And if there was a chance for something deeper, could she really risk jeopardizing her career and the campaign for it? She was starting to obsess over Max and she knew it. Lexi needed to keep her emotions in check.

"Ms. Anders?" Max's voice cut through her thoughts, snapping her back to reality. "I have a few suggestions on how security should be handled at the entrances."

"Uh, yes," Lexi stammered, pushing aside her jumbled emotions. "I see, you think we should consider adding metal detectors and checking IDs against a guest list."

"Yes, we should also liaise with the security teams for the other dignitaries that are coming. We don't want any surprises, and I'm sure they don't want any either," Max said, nodding curtly. There was no warmth in her eyes, no hint of the connection Lexi had felt moments earlier. But Lexi refused to give up hope. She knew that behind Max's icy facade might be a woman worth getting to know, and she would do everything in her power to bridge the gap between them.

"Okay, I can get you a list of the security details and numbers."

"Already done," Max said.

As they continued to work together, Lexi held on to the memory of that fleeting touch, the stolen glances that spoke volumes about her growing feelings for Max. And though Max remained distant and cold, Lexi couldn't help but wonder if maybe, just maybe, she felt it too.

Yep, she was obsessing.

⚘ ⚘ ⚘ ⚘

Max felt Lexi's gaze on her.

"Max," Hank said, snapping her back to the conversation. "You okay?"

"Of course," she replied. "Just want to make sure everything goes smoothly tonight. Make sure you and Jules are dressed to impress. I don't want you to stand out as security. Have you liaised with your counterparts from the other camps?"

"Yep, we are solid there." Hank nodded. "We've got your back."

"Thanks," Max said, appreciating the support from her team. She turned her focus back to the task at hand, determined not to let her personal feelings for Lexi affect her work. But as much as she tried to maintain a professional distance, an undeniable pull remained between them.

Later that evening, amid the bustle of final preparations for the event, Max found herself alone with Lexi in the dimly lit hallway outside the ballroom. Their eyes met, and for a brief moment the tension between them was palpable.

"Good luck tonight," Lexi said, her voice barely audible above the hum of activity around them.

"Thank you, Ms. Anders," Max replied, her gaze never leaving Lexi's.

❧ ❧ ❧ ❧

"Officer Church." Lexi hesitated, unsure of what to say next.

"Listen, let me stop you," Max began, her voice soft but resolute. "I can't pretend that everything is

fine between us. I know you think there's something...
happening here, and I think we both know that isn't an
option, right?"

Lexi swallowed hard, her eyes locked with Max's.
She could feel the unspoken truth pressing down on
them, an invisible force that threatened to shatter the
fragile professional balance they'd managed to maintain
thus far.

"We have a job to do," Max continued, her tone
firm. "This campaign is important, and I don't want
our personal conflict to interfere with it."

"Neither do I," Lexi agreed. Deflated that Max
was referring to the conflict between them and not the
sexual tension she was feeling, it felt like a confession, a
surrender to the reality of their situation. "But ignoring
it won't make it go away, either."

"No," Max admitted, sighing. "It won't. But
maybe...maybe if we agree to keep the animus to a
minimum, it will help us keep our priorities straight."

Lexi suddenly felt as if they were talking about
two different things.

"Of course," she said, her heart aching as the
distance between them seemed to stretch for miles. "Of
course. You're absolutely right."

Max hesitated, her eyes darting away from Lexi's
as she grappled with the awkward silence. At last, she
looked back at Lexi, her gaze steady and determined.
"We have to," she said, her voice laced with conviction.
"For the sake of the campaign, and for ourselves."

Lexi nodded, steeling herself for the difficult task
ahead. "We'll put the campaign first."

"Agreed," Max said, holding out her hand for Lexi
to shake. As their fingers met, Lexi felt a jolt of electricity
race through her, a reminder of the unresolved tension

that still lingered between them.

"Good luck to you tonight," Max whispered, pulling her hand away as the sound of approaching footsteps reached their ears.

"Thanks," Lexi replied, her resolve wavering as she was struck by the sudden, desperate urge to reach out and pull Max into her arms.

"Ms. Anders," Max warned, her voice low and urgent. "We need to go."

"Right." Lexi forced herself to turn away and walk down the corridor, her heart pounding in her chest.

Chapter Ten

Max sat on the hood of her car, parked by the side of a deserted road, her eyes scanning the horizon as the sun dipped below it. She needed a break from the constant noise and motion of the campaign headquarters, which could be deafening and suffocating at times. She longed for the quiet of her patrol car and the open ribbon of highways that spread out before her.

Her phone vibrated. Lexi Anders. "So much for privacy," she whispered.

"Officer Church," Lexi's voice had a strain to it Max hadn't heard before. "Congresswoman Marsh and I would like to meet with you privately as soon as possible. Can you come to the campaign office immediately?"

"Of course," Max replied, trying to keep her tone steady. She slid off the hood and got behind the wheel, wondering what could have brought about such an urgent summons.

As she drove, Max felt a stab of anxiety. Working closely with Congresswoman Marsh and Lexi Anders had presented an opportunity she wouldn't have sought out, but would it ultimately end up hurting her career? She tried to shake off her lingering doubts as she pulled up to the campaign office, steeling herself for whatever awaited her inside.

Pulling the door open, Max was greeted by Lexi,

who looked unusually solemn. "Thank you for coming so quickly, Officer Church," she said, leading her toward Congresswoman Marsh's private office.

"Of course," Max replied, her curiosity piqued.

Congresswoman Marsh stood at the window, her posture rigid. Max recognized the body language immediately.

"They sent me a letter," she finally said, her voice barely above a whisper. "I don't know who they are, but they're threatening to do something to my son Will if I don't drop out of the race. If I don't want them to release that...sensitive information."

Max could hear the fear in her voice and felt sorry for the woman. She knew the depths a mother would go to protect their child. She'd seen it firsthand on her deployment to the Middle East. Mothers with little to   nothing did everything they could to protect what they had for their children—food, shelter, their very lives. While not the same as the political problems Marsh had, the same instinct was still the same. "Do you still have the letter? When do they expect you to meet their demands?" she asked gently.

"In two weeks," Congresswoman Marsh replied, tears threatening to spill. She stood and walked to her desk, pulled open a drawer, and extracted the letter and envelope. "And if I don't comply, they've threatened to harm Will."

A pang of sympathy shot through Max, and she clenched her fists, holding back the anger at the thought of someone using a mother's love against her. She took a deep breath and let it out slowly, allowing herself a moment to focus on the task ahead. Max pulled a set of latex gloves from her inner pocket, a habit she'd acquired both as a service member and a cop. Slipping them on, she took the letter and inspected it, looking for a postmark, a stamp, anything that might help track them down.

"This letter wasn't mailed."

"No, I noticed that too," Marsh said, dabbing her eyes.

"Alright." Max forced her tone to remain calm. "The first thing we'll need to do is dust it for fingerprints and then run more extensive background checks on all staffers and anyone associated with the campaign. Someone brought this into the office. We can't afford any blind spots. Besides, we might get lucky on the fingerprints and ID the person who delivered it."

Congresswoman Marsh nodded, wiping away a stray tear. "I understand. It's difficult to think that someone close to us could be involved, but I know it's necessary."

"Clearly this came through interoffice mail. The person who wrote it and the person who dropped it off likely aren't the same person." Max squinted at the envelope as if she had some sort of superpower to detect fingerprints. She offered the congresswoman a slight, reassuring smile. She admired   Marsh's strength despite her fear, and she recognized her courage to ask for help. "We'll get you through this, Congresswoman," she reassured her. "We'll find the person responsible and put an end to this."

The determination in Max's voice seemed to offer a bit of solace to Congresswoman Marsh, who managed to give a weak smile in return.

Max promised herself that she would not rest until the blackmailer was brought to justice. She leaned against the edge of the desk, her eyes scanning the room as she considered their next move. The tension in the office was palpable, with Congresswoman Marsh's vulnerability on full display after revealing the blackmail plot. "I want the offices swept for bugs, the computers checked for malware, and I want to make sure everyone has had a background check. Are you okay with that?" She looked at Lexi and then Marsh. "I also want you to collapse your inner circle, just until the campaign is over. Someone is getting access to your office, and we have no idea who's listening or who isn't who they claim to be. I would also like everyone badged and a card reader installed at all entrances and exits."

"Won't people notice the changes and start asking questions?" Lexi interjected.

"I'm the new head of security and I'm just instituting new protocols. That should answer any questions everyone might have."

"Do you think that's necessary?" Marsh asked.

"Congresswoman, I do. I want to know who is coming and going. Also, no unauthorized guests should be allowed on site," Max began, her voice steady and determined. "We're going to need some outside help on this one. I have a contact in DC who specializes in cases like these. They can provide us with the resources we need to get to the bottom of this."

Congresswoman Marsh hesitated, wringing her hands together as she weighed the risks of involving more people in the situation. "Will they be discreet?"

"Absolutely," Max assured her. "They're highly skilled in dealing with sensitive information, and they understand the stakes involved."

"Alright," Marsh agreed, her voice barely above a whisper. "Bring them in."

Max nodded, making a mental note to reach out to her contact as soon as possible. But first, there were more immediate concerns to address.

"Before we leave this office," Max continued, her tone firm but gentle, "I want to stress the importance of keeping our conversation here completely confidential. The last thing we need is for any details about the blackmail to leak out, so I'll establish communication protocols to ensure that everything remains secure."

"Of course," Marsh replied, her eyes reflecting the heaviness of the burden she now bore. "I trust your judgment, Max."

As if sensing Lexi's concern, Max glanced over at her, offering a small, reassuring smile. It was a simple gesture, but it spoke volumes about the path they were about to embark on.

"Congresswoman Marsh." Max shifted her shoulders so she was addressing both Lexi and the congresswoman. "We're going to get through this, but we need to work together. And we need to act fast. Every minute we waste gives the blackmailers more power over us."

"Agreed," Lexi responded, her eyes filled with determination. "We're ready to do whatever it takes."

"Good." Max nodded, then turned to the congresswoman. "We should start by identifying everyone who might have had access to the information they're using against you. I'll oversee background checks on all the staffers and anyone else associated with the campaign."

"Of course, Max." Congresswoman Marsh sighed, her face etched with worry. "Whatever you need, just let me know."

Chapter Eleven

A full moon cast a dim, eerie glow over the secluded location where Lexi and Max arranged to meet. A chill ran down Lexi's spine as she surveyed the surroundings, her eyes darting around the unnerving stillness.

"Ms. Anders," Max called out in a hushed tone, emerging from the shadows like a phantom. Her features blended with the encroaching darkness, and her eyes pierced through the veil of twilight.

"Officer Church," Lexi said, her voice barely audible. "Is all this cloak-and-dagger really necessary?"

"I'm afraid so," Max replied, maintaining her low volume. "We need to discuss this blackmail scandal and figure out our next move without prying eyes, and until we have the office swept, I don't think it's wise to talk there. Trust me, they are everywhere."

"Do you know something?" Lexi asked, taking a deep breath. She couldn't help but notice the tension in Max's posture, a testament to the seriousness of the situation. "I mean, what do you know so far?"

"Congresswoman Marsh and her son, Will, are being targeted by a group of blackmailers," Max began, her voice steady despite their cautious whispers. "They're trying to force the congresswoman to resign her campaign, and they seem to have something to back up their threats."

"Okay, Captain Obvious, I know all of this," Lexi muttered, clenching her fists. "What kind of monsters are we dealing with here?"

"Actually, it's hard to say," Max admitted, her brow furrowing in concentration. "But we need to find out, and fast. I think there is someone inside feeding them information. Hence all the cloak-and-dagger stuff."

"Okay." Lexi nodded, her mind racing with possibilities. "But we can't go around and accuse people of anything. We'll need to gather proof and try to expose these people before the election. And keep the congresswoman safe, of course, if we can."

"Exactly. I'm hoping that there are fingerprints on that envelope and we can find out who delivered it. Then we would work backward to find who they are working with," Max said, her voice firm and resolute. "Remember, we need to keep this between us for now. Discretion is crucial."

"Understood," Lexi replied, her heart pounding in her chest. The urgency of their task bore down on her like a leaden shroud, but she would not let it crush her.

"Good." Max took a step closer to Lexi. "If you have questions for me, now's the time to bring them forward."

As Max spoke in hushed tones, the shadows around them seemed to deepen, as though the darkness itself were closing in on them. The first few drops of rain began to fall, spattering the ground around them as they stood in the secluded clearing. The atmosphere had grown heavy with tension, and the threat of a downpour mirrored the gravity of their conversation.

"Ms. Anders." Max's whisper was nearly drowned out by the wind rustling through the trees. "As I said before I'm bringing someone else in on this. Someone I trust completely."

"Who?"

"Sam Cork, my old military buddy. He specializes in counterterrorism," Max explained, watching Lexi's expression closely for any sign of objection.

Lexi hesitated for a moment, trying to keep up with the new developments. She knew that involving more people could increase the risk of exposure, but at the same time, she recognized the value of having an expert like Sam on their side. Finally, Lexi nodded her agreement, her eyes meeting Max's. "Alright. If you trust him, then so do I."

"I trusted him with my life when I was in the desert," Max said. "We need all the help we can get, and Sam is the best. We'll be lucky if he agrees."

"Officer Church, I'm...I'm worried about what we might be up against," Lexi admitted, her voice trembling slightly. "These people are dangerous, and we're putting ourselves—and those we care about—at risk."

"We didn't start this, Ms. Anders. Someone else decided to do that for us. Now, we play offense." Max reached out and gently squeezed her shoulder, the warmth of her touch reassuring even through the thin fabric of Lexi's shirt. "We'll take every precaution necessary. We'll do everything in our power to keep Congresswoman Marsh, Will, and ourselves safe."

As Lexi looked into Max's eyes, she saw the unyielding strength that had drawn her to the former soldier in the first place. It was a strength that made her feel secure, even in the face of seemingly insurmountable odds.

"Promise me," Lexi whispered, her heart pounding in her chest as she sought solace in Max's unwavering determination.

"I promise, Lexi. I won't let anything happen to the people we're trying to protect." Max's voice was steady and strong despite the storm brewing around them.

In that moment, something shifted in Lexi. Max had used Lexi's name and dropped the formality, forging a connection. As the rain began to fall lightly, Lexi leaned in close enough to feel Max's breath against her cheek.

"Okay, what can I do? I know everyone at the office and have a lot of background on Will. I think I can help," Lexi said as the first rumble of distant thunder echoed through the trees.

"Agreed," Max replied, moving away from Lexi. Her eyes filled with a fierce determination that sent a shiver down Lexi's spine.

"Discretion is essential," Max continued, her voice barely audible above the soft patter of raindrops against the leaves above them. "We can't risk spooking anyone or tipping off anyone working with the blackmailers. You'll have to ask questions without really asking them. Understand?"

"Of course," Lexi agreed. Her mind was already racing through potential witnesses and how she might approach each one. She knew that gaining their trust would be crucial if they wanted to uncover the truth behind this sordid affair.

"I can't ask questions I don't know the answer to, but you can. We are going to need a way to communicate securely. I don't recommend using texts or phone calls, so those are now off-limits for the group. An encrypted messaging app should suffice, but we'll need to be extra cautious."

"Right," Lexi murmured, her gaze following Max's

as she searched the shadows for any hint of danger. It was unsettling to know that someone was going to such great lengths to ruin Will and Congresswoman Marsh, and she couldn't help but wonder what other sinister plans they had in store.

"Another thing," Max said, her tone growing more serious. "We'll need surveillance equipment. Hidden cameras, tracking devices, anything that can help us gather evidence without being detected."

"Where do we even get that kind of stuff?" Lexi asked, her brow furrowing in concern.

"I have a few contacts I can reach out to," Max replied, her eyes narrowing. "I trust them implicitly, but we still need to take precautions."

"Alright," Lexi conceded, swallowing hard.

"Lexi," Max said softly, reaching out to gently grasp her hand. "I know this is a lot to take in, but I promise you, you'll get through this."

For a moment, Lexi allowed herself to be swept up in the warmth of Max's touch, then she dropped her hand. She knew that too much personal contact wasn't good for an operation. It blinded a person to the stakes at hand, and she needed Max to stay on her A-game.

"Thank you," Lexi whispered. Her jaw tightened as she thought about what they were about to face. The possibilities were many and varied, but if they couldn't identify the blackmailers, it all rested on whether these people were willing to take their threats to the next level. And that possibility scared the hell out of Lexi.

≈≈≈≈

Sam arrived in the city the next day, and they had agreed that he should meet them at Lexi's place after work so they could start to plan the operation. Max had made it clear that the security team needed to be part of the process. Keeping them in the dark would tie one hand behind their back, and right now they needed all the eyes they could get.

"Before we bring the rest of the team in on this," Max said, her voice low and steady, "we need a solid plan in place. We can't afford any loose ends."

"Okay," Lexi replied. "But what about the surveillance equipment we talked about?"

"Let me handle that," Max assured her, a determined glint in her eyes. "I have connections that can get us what we need without raising any red flags."

Lexi nodded. She'd come to trust Max's skill in this area implicitly. From her careful and discreet planning to the way she had swept her home for listening devices, Max had proven to be as proficient as her resume promised. As Lexi ran a hand through her brown hair, her thoughts drifted toward Congresswoman Marsh and Will, whose fates now rested on their shoulders.

As if sensing her concern, Max reached out and squeezed Lexi's shoulder reassuringly. "Don't worry, we'll get them out of this mess. Just focus on what you do best: gathering information and connecting the dots."

"Right," Lexi murmured, her resolve returning as she pushed her fears aside. Her foot bounced nervously as she listened to Max go through the details of the operation.

A knock on the door startled her, and Lexi's heart skipped a beat. Max, on the other hand, was calm and resolute. Clearly, little rattled her. Peeking through the peephole, Lexi saw a mail carrier. She'd rarely had any interactions with her mailman since she got most of her mail at the campaign office.

"Package for Alexandra Anders," he announced, his voice muffled by the thick door.

Max lifted her finger to her lips and motioned Lexi away from the door.

"Thank you," Max replied as she opened the door just enough to thrust her hand out to accept the package.

"Is that how you greet   a friend?"

"You son of a bitch. How did you know I'd be here early?" Max opened the door fully and held up her hand. "Don't answer that."

"I have my ways." The man smiled and looked over at Lexi. His eyes twinkled in an odd sort of way. "I'm Sam, a friend of this nut bar. Did you order something?" he said, handing Lexi the box left on her porch. "Hi, Sam. I'm Lexi Anders, Congresswoman Marsh's campaign manager."

"Nice to meet you. Wish I could say I've heard lots about you, but that would be a lie."

"Sam..." Max sat back down. "Have a seat. So, you didn't order anything, Lexi?"

Lexi shook her head, her heart pounding in her chest as she tore open the brown paper wrapping before Max could say anything. Inside was a compact disc, its black plastic casing stark against the white label that bore her name. A shiver ran down her spine as she realized what it might contain.

As they inserted the CD into Lexi's computer, the screen flickered to life, revealing grainy footage of past campaign events involving Lexi, Congresswoman Marsh, and Will. The images were haunting, like ghosts from the past. Though the moments captured were innocent, the context in which they were now viewing them made her heart race with apprehension.

"Who would send this? It's completely benign," Lexi wondered aloud, her hands wringing together nervously.

"More importantly," Max added, her sharp gaze never leaving the screen. "Why did they send it?"

They exchanged a look as the video continued to play, each second of the innocuous footage bringing them no closer to the truth.

Her heart raced as the video tape neared its end. The images of her, Congresswoman Marsh, and Will were now replaced by a masked figure. "Congresswoman Marsh," the figure spoke in a low, menacing tone, the voice distorted to hide their identity. "We have evidence of your son's illegal activities. If you do not withdraw from the campaign and make a public statement admitting his guilt and yours, both he and you will suffer the consequences." A gun rose into view and shot at something. The camera panned to a cat lying dead on the ground. "I'm sure we've made our point."

Lexi watched as Max and Sam leaned in closer to the screen, scanning for any clue that could lead them to the blackmailer's identity.

"Whoever this is, they're playing a dangerous game," Sam muttered, his jaw tight with anger.

Max nodded in agreement, but her focus remained on the screen. "There has to be something we can use to track them down."

As the video ended, Lexi felt a cold sweat break out on her forehead. The threat was real, and it was clear that the blackmailer was following everyone involved in the campaign.

"We need to act fast," she said, her voice urgent. "We can't let them hurt Congresswoman Marsh or

Will."

"Agreed," Max replied, already pulling out her phone to make a call. "I'll contact Hank and Jules to see if they can help us with any info on the footage, and I'll get the surveillance going. We need to gather as much evidence as possible before we can take this to the authorities."

"But who are we going to surveil? We don't know who's involved."

Max looked at Lexi and asked, "Who's consistently missing in that video?"

Lexi shook her head. She had no idea who Max was referring to.

"Jenny," Max said.

"Jenny? You must be kidding. She's Will's girlfriend, she loves him. They're supposed to get married after the election."

"Being his girlfriend doesn't make her automatically an ally here," Max said before she and Sam got on their phones to set the surveillance operation in motion.

Lexi contemplated this as they finished their calls. Max had a point, but it wasn't an easy leap to peg Jenny as being involved in the blackmail plot. Plus, there were lots of possible reasons why she wasn't in the video. Maybe she hadn't attended one of the events shown. Maybe she'd been in the restroom. Worst, maybe Jenny herself was a victim of the blackmailers as well. There had to be some sort of explanation.

"Time is not on our side. The clock is ticking, and I'm worried something will happen before we can get a bead on who these people are," Lexi said, her voice barely above a whisper. She clenched her fists, feeling the urgency of their investigation weighing down on her shoulders. "We need to act quickly if we want to keep Congresswoman Marsh and Will safe."

"Agreed," Sam replied, his brow furrowed in deep concentration. "We'll need to track down every possible lead, no matter how small or insignificant it may seem. And we'll have to do it all while staying under the radar."

Max nodded, her eyes filled with determination. "I'll reach out to some contacts I trust within the law enforcement community. They might be able to help us gather intel without attracting too much attention. Plus, both Hank and Jules have intelligence backgrounds, so they will be assets once we read them in on what's happening."

Lexi nodded, but her mind was racing. This was far more serious than she'd imagined.

❧ ❧ ❧ ❧

The three of them huddled together in the dimly lit room, their eyes glued to the flickering screen as the video played out before them. The images were grainy, but there was no mistaking the familiar scenes from past campaign events.

"Pause it," Max said suddenly. Lexi hit the pause button, and they all leaned closer to the screen, examining the frozen image. "Right there." Max pointed at a figure standing near the edge of the frame. "Do you see that?"

She squinted, trying to make out the details of the person's face. It was difficult to discern any distinguishing features, but there was something undeniably familiar about the way the person stood, the confident tilt of their chin. She glanced over at

Sam, who was studying the image with an intensity that matched her own. "What do you think, Sam? Do you recognize them?"

Sam shook his head slowly, his brow furrowed in concentration. "I can't be certain, but there's definitely something…off about this person."

"Off how?" Lexi asked.

Max bit her lip, her eyes never leaving the screen. "I don't know. It's just a gut feeling, maybe, but I feel like I've seen them before. Look, I've learned to trust my instincts in situations like these." She paused, her gaze meeting Lexi's.

"Alright," Lexi said. Then, she gasped. "Max, could it be one of the blackmailers?"

"Maybe," Max replied, her voice laced with uncertainty. "We need to find out more about this person, though. There must be something that ties them to the blackmail plot."

The room was silent for a moment as they all considered the implications. Max's thoughts drifted to Congresswoman Marsh and Will, and she felt a surge of protectiveness well up inside her. She knew that time was running out, and they needed to act quickly to ensure their safety.

"Alright," Sam said finally, breaking the tense silence. "Let's keep watching. Maybe there's more we can learn from the rest of the tape."

As the video continued to play, the face of the mysterious figure haunted her, taunting her with his secrets. The tape reached its chilling conclusion, with the masked face issuing its sinister threat, and when she glanced over at Lexi, she saw her own determination mirrored in the other woman's eyes.

Chapter Twelve

L exi scanned the small hotel suite as she and Max hauled in their equipment. They'd rented it once they determined that it was likely a much safer option than setting up headquarters at Lexi's place. The room was cramped, but it would serve its purpose as a temporary base of operations away from the campaign offices. Sam followed behind them, lugging an oversized duffel bag filled with surveillance gear.

"Alright," Max said, setting down her load with a sigh. "Let's get this place set up."

Sam busied himself with organizing the various cables and electronics they'd need for their investigation. Max set up the monitors. Lexi, for her part, arranged photos and screenshots on a whiteboard they could use to visualize their progress. In just over an hour, the suite was fully functional.

Max and Sam turned to Lexi, ready to share the information they had gathered so far. Max spoke up first, her voice steady and deliberate. "We've managed to identify the figure in the video as Jose Guevara, a known drug cartel kingpin."

"Jesus," Lexi muttered under her breath, feeling a chill run through her veins at the thought of such a dangerous player being involved in the blackmail plot against Congresswoman Marsh.

"Unfortunately, that's not all," Sam added, his voice tinged with worry. "We've also discovered a possible connection between the goons they hired and

Tom Horton, a counterterrorism expert who seems to have gone rogue. He might be expecting a big payday and political clout if this plan works."

Lexi clenched her fists in frustration. She knew that every new piece of information only made this case more complex and dangerous, but she couldn't back down now. It was too important.

"Sam, do we have any leads on the connection between Guevara and Horton?" Lexi asked, her voice tense, her mind racing with possible scenarios. She glanced at Max, seeking assurance.

"Nothing concrete yet," Sam admitted, running a hand through his hair. "But we're working on it."

Max stepped in, sensing Lexi's growing concern. "We'll figure it out, Lexi. We've got a solid team here, and we're all committed to getting to the truth and protecting Congresswoman Marsh's campaign." She placed a reassuring hand on Lexi's shoulder, igniting a warmth in Lexi that extended far beyond the physical touch.

"Thanks, Max," Lexi said softly, feeling ever so slightly more grounded. The stakes were high, and the risks even higher, but Max had a confidence that rubbed off on her. At least she hoped that was what she was feeling.

☙ ☙ ❧ ❧

"Alright," Max began, her voice steady and determined. "Based on what we know so far, we need to gather more evidence without tipping our hand or putting Congresswoman Marsh at risk. Here's what I propose." She uncapped the marker, the scent of ink filling the air, and began sketching out their plan.

"First, we need to confirm who this unidentified male with Guevara is," Max said, drawing a figure on the board. "He could be the key to understanding the connection between the blackmailers and the drug cartel."

"Agreed," Lexi said. "But how do we get close enough to him without raising suspicions?"

"Discreet surveillance," Max replied, scribbling notes beside the figure, her mind racing with possible avenues of investigation. "We'll use hidden cameras and stakeouts to track his movements and gather intel."

Lexi frowned, her gaze clouded with worry. "And if he spots us? What then?"

"Then we adapt," Max answered firmly, meeting Lexi's gaze with unwavering confidence. "But we won't let it come to that. We'll be cautious and strategic." She glanced at Sam, who nodded in agreement.

"Okay." Lexi sighed. "What's next?"

Max turned back to the whiteboard, outlining further steps. "While we focus on the unidentified man, we'll also continue monitoring Jenny's activities. That's Will's girlfriend, right? That brings me to this." She pulled out a set of photos and pasted them onto the board.

"Why Jenny?"

"Well, surveillance is paying off already. We've got pictures of Jenny meeting with different people." Max pointed to two of the photos. "These are a surprise – Congresswoman Marsh's opponent, Dan Brown." The images showed Dan passing envelopes to Jenny, their faces betraying no emotion.

"Damn," Lexi muttered, her voice a tight tangle of anger. "I knew he was ruthless, but this…"

"Unfortunately, it gets worse." Max continued,

revealing another set of photos where Jenny handed those same envelopes to the unidentified Mexican male. "There's clearly a connection between Dan Brown and the blackmailers."

"Which means we're up against more than just a few rogue criminals," Lexi said, clearly dejected.

Max felt for Lexi, her heart sinking. It was clear that the stakes were higher than Lexi had ever imagined, the responsibility pressed down upon her. Max knew she and Sam were the only things standing in the way of not only the ruin of Marsh's reelection, but also the demolition of Lexi's career—and, if things went truly sideways, possibly even her life. She couldn't quite put her finger on why she was so drawn to Alexandra Anders, but the way the attraction grew as each day passed unsettled her brain even as her heart longed to give in to the allure of the brilliant campaign manager.

In the quiet moments between action and planning, Max felt the spark of something more than camaraderie, an undercurrent of attraction that simmered just beneath the surface. She was pretty sure that Lexi felt it too, but she pushed the thought away. There was no room for such feelings in a situation like this. Instead, she focused on their mission, steeling herself for what was to come. There would be many trials ahead, and the last thing she needed was a romantic entanglement with someone she was supposed to be protecting.

⚓⚓⚓⚓

"Alright, let's start again with what we know for sure," Lexi said, her eyes narrowed in concentration. She drew a timeline on the board, marking off key events—Jenny's meetings with Dan Brown, the exchanges with the unidentified man, and all the other significant incidents they had uncovered during their investigation.

Max nodded, her eyes intense as she scrutinized the data. "We need to find the connecting thread between all these players. It's the only way we'll be able to expose their schemes."

Lexi couldn't help but admire Max's unwavering determination, even in the face of such daunting odds. She felt a surge of affection for the strong, resolute woman beside her.

"Let's look for patterns," Lexi suggested. Patterns were her stock-in-trade. They could tell her how people would vote based on location, education, and socioeconomics. Her heart rate accelerated at the proximity of Max's body heat. "Maybe there are specific days or locations that can give us more insight into their operations."

As they pored over the evidence together, Lexi found herself increasingly drawn to Max's keen intellect and analytical mind. Their late-night strategy sessions were charged with an electric energy that sent shivers down Lexi's spine, making it difficult to focus on anything other than the undeniable chemistry between them.

"Hey, I've got an idea," Lexi said suddenly, her heart pounding as she turned to face Max. "Why don't we reach out to potential witnesses or sources who might have information about this blackmail plot and question them? I mean, I didn't get a lot from the staff, so maybe we'll get some more information from people who don't work for the campaign but do attend the events."

Max considered this for a moment, her gaze

never leaving Lexi's. "That sounds like a logical idea, but how do we do it without alerting them? If you can come up with a way, that would be great. Meanwhile, I'll focus on analyzing the video footage and identifying any potential leads on the periphery of the key players. It'll be like casting a wider net—we're bound to catch something."

"Exactly," Lexi agreed, her breath hitching as Max's hand brushed against hers, the fleeting contact sending a jolt of electricity through her body.

Lexi watched as Max took control of the room. She commanded attention and respect, and Lexi was drawn to strong, confident women. Those qualities were her kryptonite.

♫ ♫ ♫ ♫

Lexi leaned against the edge of the table, her fingers drumming a nervous rhythm on the surface. The hotel suite was dimly lit, creating an atmosphere that in most other circumstances could have seemed romantic. But these weren't other circumstances, and the ambient lighting only served to enhance the feeling of mystery and danger. Photos and documents were strewn about, a patchwork of evidence that seemed to defy logic at times. The light from a computer screen cast an eerie glow on Max's face as she stared at it intently.

"Max," Lexi began, her voice tense with urgency. "We've got to ensure Congresswoman Marsh's campaign remains intact. I think Jenny is the key link between Dan Brown's campaign and the drug dealer. There's no telling what they might do if they realize we're closing in."

Max nodded, her eyes reflecting the importance of the situation. "Right. We have to tread carefully and avoid making any missteps that could jeopardize our investigation or the congresswoman's campaign."

"Exactly." Lexi chewed on her lower lip, her mind racing with possibilities. "I think we should look at Will and Jenny's time in college. Maybe some of his buddies saw something or know something that can help us put the pieces together. This all started when Will was in college, so it only makes sense to go back to the beginning. His college days."

As Lexi spoke, Max's gaze lingered on her face. Thank God the room was dark, as she could feel her face flush at the stare

"Let's talk about the risks," Max said, her tone somber. "We could be diving headfirst into some dangerous territory, Lexi. The deeper we go into this twisted world of politics, blackmail, and drugs, the more we expose ourselves to threats."

Lexi glanced down, her hands trembling slightly as she acknowledged the reality of the situation. "I know, but we have to do this, Max. For Congresswoman Marsh, for Will, and for everyone who's counting on us to get to the truth."

"Of course," Max agreed, her voice softening. "But we need to be smart about it. We have to watch our backs and make sure we're not putting ourselves in unnecessary danger. I'm not going to lie, it could be dangerous. The drug cartels are notorious for their savage way of dealing with problems."

"Okay. What are you saying?"

Max looked over at Sam, hoping for some help. "I think you should back out."

"What? No. I told the congresswoman that I

would help."

"And you have. I can't guarantee your safety, Lexi."

A heavy silence hung between them, punctuated only by the distant hum of traffic outside the hotel room. Lexi could feel   Max's concern, and she appreciated her willingness to protect her from the risk, but she wasn't about to bail now.

"She's right, Lexi. You're not trained to tackle something like this. Even on a good day, those of us who are trained might not come out unscathed. We know the risks," Sam said.

"I'm not taking any risk. I'm just doing what I do best—read the data, get the information, and keep the coffee cups warm."

"Look, they sent that CD to you, not Congresswoman Marsh. They didn't mail it, they didn't send it via messenger service, they walked it to your door, Lexi. Why do you think they did that?"

"Because..." she started, and Max finished.

"Because you're her campaign manager. They know you're connected to Marsh. You know Will. They want you to convince the congresswoman to drop out, because you are the only one who could sway her to do so."

"But I wouldn't do that."

Max looked at Sam and then back to Lexi. "Wouldn't you, though? To protect her and Will?"

Lexi looked down at her hands. "I don't know."

Max looked at her, clearly skeptical. "Lexi—"

"Look, I'll leave the GI Jane stuff to you guys. Don't kick me from the team, Max. I want to help. Besides, I'll be asking you all kinds of questions and worrying if you bench me. If I promise to back out when it gets crazy...."

Max reached for Lexi's hand, the warmth of their intertwined fingers offering a semblance of comfort amid the chaos. "This is getting dangerous. I don't want to have to worry about any civilians that might get in the way. We need to be focused on the mission, and with the drug cartel involved, they already know you're potentially another target, which is an asset to them. Will, Congresswoman Marsh...heck, all of you are in the crosshairs."

"I appreciate your concern, but I can take care of myself, Max."

⁂

Max stood at the window, her gaze fixed on the bustling streets. The city was alive with movement, each passerby unaware of the sinister plot unfolding in their midst. She turned back to face Lexi and Sam.

"Listen, we need to stay under the radar," Max said firmly. "The last thing we want is to tip off the blackmailers that we're on to them."

Lexi nodded, her brow furrowed in concentration. "You're right. We can't afford any slip-ups." She hesitated for a moment before continuing. "What about Hank and Jules? Should we bring them closer into the investigation?"

Max considered the question, weighing the pros and cons. "I think they should know what's going on, but their primary focus should be on protecting Marsh. The goons could just be looking for an opening to grab her."

"Okay," Lexi replied, her jaw set in determination. "So we keep them on a need-to-know basis but make sure the congresswoman's safety is their top priority. You yourself said their training was an asset for us, but I don't see them being used to their full potential, and we are running out of time."

Max stared at Lexi, stunned into silence. She couldn't argue with that logic, and the sight of Lexi's passion and fiery indignation stirred a reaction she hadn't felt in a long time. She was decidedly, unexpectedly, turned on. She shook the feeling away and put on her professional mask as quickly as she could, only nodding her agreement in return. She took a deep breath to center herself and was relieved when Lexi's attention turned back to the case.

With that settled, the trio dove into the daunting task before them. They spent long hours together, poring over documents, analyzing data, and brainstorming strategies trying to uncover the truth behind the blackmail plot.

Max found herself immersed in a sea of information, her mind racing as she pieced together connections and patterns. Beside her, Sam's tactical expertise was proving invaluable, his keen instincts guiding their analysis in the right direction.

As the hours ticked by, the room seemed to grow smaller, the walls closing in around them. Max was starting to feel the seriousness of the investigation bearing down on her, threatening to suffocate her if she let it. But then she would glance over at Lexi, her resolve a steady anchor amid the storm, and she could breathe again.

❧ ❧ ❧ ❧

Lexi sat at the small table in their hotel suite,

surrounded by piles of documents and half-empty coffee cups. Her eyes were bleary from hours of staring at the same words over and over again, her mind buzzing with the details of the case. Their days were spent campaigning, their nights hip-deep in blackmail.

Max was sitting across from her, her expression serious as she scanned through another report. Despite the tension in the air, Lexi couldn't help but feel a sense of comfort in Max's presence.

"Hey," Max said suddenly, breaking the silence. "You look like you could use a break."

Lexi nodded gratefully, standing up and stretching her stiff muscles. As they made their way to the small kitchenette, Lexi couldn't help but notice how clean and organized Max kept the space. It was a stark contrast to the chaos of their investigation, a reminder of the order that Max brought into her life.

"Thanks for this," Lexi said, taking a sip of her coffee. "I don't know how I would have gotten through this without more coffee."

Max smiled softly, her eyes shining with warmth. "Same here."

Lexi felt a shiver down her spine at the intensity of Max's gaze. It was as if she was seeing straight through Lexi's defenses, peeling back the layers of her soul to reveal the raw vulnerability beneath.

"Listen," Max said suddenly, her voice low and urgent.

Lexi felt her heart rate spike, wondering what Max needed to say. They had been working shoulder to shoulder for the past week, and yet there was still so much that Lexi wanted to ask Max.

"Max," she said, barely able to get the words out. "I want to apologize for bringing you into this mess."

"Seriously? Look, we need to focus like a laser. Right now, all I'm thinking about is getting through the next few days." Max avoided looking at Lexi.

Deflated, Lexi said, "I understand."

≈ ≈ ≈ ≈

The heavy rain drummed against the small hotel suite's windows, a constant reminder of the storm brewing outside of their temporary base, but it also seemed like a metaphor for the last week.

Chaos.

Lexi stood by the window, watching as droplets slid down the glass like tiny rivers, her thoughts consumed by the web of deceit and danger they were all entangled in. How had things become so twisted and warped? She was just a campaign manager, and now she was playing super sleuth trying to expose a blackmail plot to save her boss's campaign.

"Hey." Max's voice cut through the silence, warm and steady despite the gravity of their situation. "We've been at this for hours. You need to eat something."

Lexi turned around to find Max holding out a takeout container, a slight smile on her lips. Their eyes met, and Lexi felt that familiar heat rise up within her.

Stay focused, she told herself. Max wasn't on the menu.

"Thanks," Lexi replied, taking the food with a nod. They sat down at the small table in the corner of the room, their knees brushing beneath it as they ate in companionable silence.

"Tell me about your family," Max suddenly asked, breaking the stillness. The question caught Lexi off guard, but she welcomed the opportunity to think about something other than the case.

"Uh, well, my parents are both professors, so our household was always filled with books and debates," Lexi began, a fond smile forming on her face. "I have an older brother who's a lawyer, and a younger sister who's studying art history."

"Sounds like a smart bunch," Max said, her interest seeming to be genuine.

"Too smart for our own good sometimes." Lexi chuckled. She looked at Max expectantly, urging her to share her own story. "What about you?"

Max hesitated for a moment before saying anything. "My dad was an army officer, so we moved around a lot when I was a kid. My mom...she passed away when I was young." Her voice wavered, and Lexi reached over to squeeze her hand, offering a silent gesture of comfort.

"Sorry to hear that," Lexi whispered, her heart aching for Max's loss. "You must really miss her."

"Every day," Max admitted, her eyes glistening with unshed tears. But she shook off the emotion and continued. "I have an older sister who's a nurse, and a younger brother who just went back to college."

"Seems like we both come from families of overachievers," Lexi teased gently, trying to lighten the mood.

"Guess so," Max agreed, the hint of a smile returning to her face.

The rain outside had lessened to a soft patter, but Lexi knew the storm was coming. She only hoped that they could save the campaign and expose Brown for the bastard he was. Her mom had always told her that she was more of a glass-half-full kinda kid. Hopefully, she was right.

Chapter Thirteen

"Max," Lexi said, her eyes filled with worry. "We can't keep this from Congresswoman Marsh any longer. She has to know." Lexi tapped the CD. They had waited a couple of days, hoping to be able to add more context to the threat or at least find out who had sent it, but they'd hit a brick wall. Will's college buddies had helped piece Will's uni days together—mostly drunken weekends—but two things they all said was that Jenny had been a permanent fixture on his arm, and that Will brought the party to the party. Meaning, he brought the drugs, and then he suddenly started dealing to feed his own habit. It was an easy sell, as there was no lack of eager partakers. These particular rich college kids had an endless supply of cash and the ever-present need to party like rockstars. Jenny was the X factor in everything. She fit, most certainly, but they just didn't know how—yet.

Max sighed. "I know, Lexi. I just…I don't want to be responsible for distracting her from the campaign. She hired me to handle all of these things so she didn't have to think about them."

Lexi stepped closer, her hand reaching out to touch Max's arm. "We're doing what's best for both her and Will. This is bigger than the campaign now. It's about keeping them safe."

Max hesitated, her gaze lingering on Lexi's determined face. She knew Lexi was right, but the consequences of their decision bore down on her shoulders like a ton of bricks. They were about to tell Marsh more about her son than she probably wanted to know.

"Alright," Max agreed, her voice barely above a whisper. "Let's arrange the meeting."

⚜⚜⚜⚜

Lexi waved her badge at the door and entered Congresswoman Marsh's outer office. Max noticed Sarah, the press secretary, typing furiously at her computer, while Ethan, the chief of staff, sucked on his signature flavored vape pen, seemingly oblivious to the heavy tension that hung in the air as he packed up his belongings for the night.

"Is the congresswoman available? It's urgent," Lexi asked.

"Hey, Lexi. Let me check," Sarah replied, her sharp smile not quite reaching her eyes. She picked up the phone and dialed the congresswoman's extension. "Congresswoman Marsh, Lexi and Max are here to see you. They say it's urgent...Yes...Yes, I understand. Thank you, and good night to you as well. I'll see you in the morning." She hung up and gestured toward the large oak door. "Go ahead."

Max's breath caught in her throat as she stepped into the congresswoman's office. The walls were lined with shelves filled with books, civic awards, and framed photographs, a testament to the life of a dedicated public servant. Lexi followed closely behind, her presence a source of comfort for Max as she thought about the storm they were about to unleash.

"Lexi, Max," Congresswoman Marsh greeted them, her carefully polished smile betraying no hint of the turmoil that awaited her. "Do you have news?"

"Congresswoman Marsh," Max began, her voice wavering slightly. "We do. It's about your campaign and...your son."

As she spoke, Max couldn't help but think of the potential fallout from their revelation. The consequences could be disastrous, but there was no turning back now. The truth had to come out.

"Have a seat," Marsh replied, gesturing to the couch in her office, her eyes narrowing with concern as she joined them. "Tell me everything."

The door clicked shut behind them, sealing Lexi and Max inside the sun-drenched office. Marsh studied their faces, her eyes searching for clues about the matter at hand. The air grew thick with anticipation, a palpable silence enveloping the room.

"Congresswoman," Lexi began, her voice steady despite the gravity of what she was about to reveal. "We've uncovered extensive evidence of the blackmail plot against you and your campaign. It involves a drug cartel, your opponent Dan Brown, and...your son's girlfriend, Jenny."

The congresswoman's face paled as the depth of the blackmail plot sank in. "That bastard Dan Brown is involved...I knew it. He'll do anything to win." Congresswoman Marsh shook her head, and Max wondered if she'd missed the reference to Will's girlfriend.

Max handed over a folder containing photographs and documents they'd gathered during their investigation. Marsh flipped through the pages, her fingers trembling ever so slightly. She looked up at Lexi and Max, her eyes wide with shock and fear.

"Are you certain of this?"

"Absolutely," Max replied. "We've followed every lead, cross-checked every piece of information. It all points to a coordinated effort to bring you down and destroy your campaign."

As the congresswoman continued to process the information, her gaze fell upon a photograph of Will, his carefree grin a stark contrast to the grim reality he unknowingly had entangled himself and his mother in.

"Is he...is Will in danger?" she whispered, her voice quivering.

"We believe he's being used as a pawn," Lexi said softly, offering a sympathetic smile. "But we don't have any evidence that he's directly involved in the plot."

"Then we must act quickly," the congresswoman declared, determination flickering in her eyes like a newly kindled flame. "We can't let them hurt my son or destroy everything we've worked so hard for."

Max pulled the CD from her jacket. "Can I borrow your computer?"

Marsh nodded.

Max pushed the disc in and pushed play, spun the computer around, and the three of them watched the video.

Marsh covered her mouth. "I can't believe this."

"It's clear they will go to any lengths to get you to drop out," Max said, ejecting the disc.

"I think we should call in the FBI," Lexi said.

"We can't." She looked at Max. "Can't you catch them?"

"Well, we don't have enough to take to the police."

"I won't file a police report, Max. I can't."

Max sighed. "I'm straddling a fine line here, Congresswoman."

"I understand. I really do. But this could all be for

nothing. We can call their bluff, can't we?"

"We could." Max said, looking at Lexi and hoping she would try to convince the congresswoman to do the right thing and involve the authorities.

"Then we do that." Marsh stood and walked to her desk. "As you said, we don't have enough evidence to accuse Dan Brown. It's his word against mine."

"True." Max nodded. "We have a plan to catch them, but it won't be easy."

"Whatever it takes." Congresswoman Marsh's voice was firm. "I will not let these criminals destroy my family or my campaign."

The tension in the room gradually began to dissipate with that declaration, replaced by a sense of urgency.

Lexi pushed a strand of her brown hair behind her ear, her eyes encouraging as she looked to Max to explain the best way to proceed.

"Congresswoman, we have a plan to catch Jenny red-handed, gathering more evidence against her and putting an end to this whole scheme."

"Go on," Congresswoman Marsh urged, her voice wavering slightly with apprehension.

Max stepped forward as she tucked her hair neatly behind her ears, eyes focused intently on the congresswoman. "You have a campaign event coming up. We think that this is probably a good time to confront Jenny. If we do it in a public place, I don't think she's going to want to make a scene. We know she'll be there with Will. Lexi pulls her to the side and questions her." She paused, gauging the congresswoman's reaction. "We'll be watching the entire time, ready to step in when necessary."

Fear was evident in the creased lines of Marsh's

forehead. "What if Jenny goes to the press and exposes everything before the event? It could ruin the campaign…and my son."

"Congresswoman, we understand your concerns," Lexi said, her tone even and measured. "But if we don't act now, the consequences could be far worse. These guys will continue to hold power over you, and there's no telling what they might do next."

"Jenny's a loose cannon," Max added, her practiced expression honed from her years in the military. "If we don't confront her, she could bring this entire operation crashing down around us. The blackmailers have given you a deadline, so we are on a tight timeline. My people will be stationed throughout the event. If anything goes sideways, we'll get you and Will out of there, quick."

Marsh closed her eyes for a moment and took a deep breath. The air in the room felt thick, heavy with the burden of responsibility that lay squarely on her shoulders.

"Are you sure Will isn't involved in any way? I'm just having a really hard time wrapping my head around all of this." The vulnerability in Marsh's eyes spoke volumes about the fear that surely gnawed at her core.

Max shrugged her shoulders, offering the slightest hint of reassurance. "We haven't found any evidence that he's involved. He's just an unknowing pawn in the blackmail scheme. These people are vultures, and they are just exploiting him and his past."

As Lexi and Max continued to make their case, it became clear just how high the stakes were. This wasn't just a game of political volleying; it was a battle for their very lives, and they had to be willing to fight tooth and nail to emerge victorious.

"Please, Congresswoman," Lexi implored. "If you won't call in the FBI, you'll have to trust that Max and her team can get this done."

The congresswoman's office seemed to close in around them, the polished mahogany desk and towering bookshelves bearing witness to the high-stakes conversation unfolding within their confines. The faint hum of traffic outside the window underscored the urgency of the moment, a reminder of the world that waited just beyond these walls—a world that hung in the balance as Lexi and Max made their final plea.

"Think carefully about it, Congresswoman. Reconsider calling in the feds," Max urged. She clenched her fists, knuckles turning white as she fought to control her emotions. "Not only is your career on the line, but so are the lives of innocent people who have no idea they're being used as pawns in this sick game."

Congresswoman Marsh's eyes darted between Lexi and Max, her lips pressed into a thin line.

"Your integrity has always been one of your greatest assets, Congresswoman," Lexi continued, her words cutting through the tension like a knife. "This is your chance to prove that you stand for justice, even when it means putting yourself and your loved ones at risk. If you let this plot go unchecked, you're not only betraying your own principles, but the trust of the people who believe in you."

Silence stretched between them, heavy with the unspoken fears and the knowledge that the decision Max was asking Congresswoman Marsh to make could alter the course of her life forever. The air itself seemed to hold its breath, waiting for the moment when she would either rise to meet the challenge before her or crumble beneath the pressure. Max could see that

Marsh was choosing her words carefully.

"Involving formal law enforcement at this moment is too risky. The more people who know, the greater the chances are that it will be leaked. Worse, the wrong person knowing could screw the whole thing up. It just takes one idiot looking for a payday to bring the whole thing down in flames. I'm putting my trust in you two and your judgment. Just keep my son safe and nail these bastards. If there are consequences later, I'll take them."

As they prepared to leave the office, Max caught Lexi's eye, her expression a mixture of relief and apprehension. In that brief glance, something unspoken passed between them—a promise, perhaps, or a reaffirmation of the bond that had grown stronger with each passing day.

"I understand," Max murmured, her words sounding more resolved than she believed. She'd felt this type of combat claustrophobia before. There was no good way to turn so she had to move forward, and that meant taking a risk. She hated that part of her military service. She could handle whatever happened to her, but when civilians were involved, it made for difficult decisions.

With a final nod to Congresswoman Marsh, Lexi and Max turned on their heels and strode out of the office, each step echoing through the hushed space. The door clicked shut behind them, sealing off the air of vulnerability that had permeated the room just moments before. The outer office was empty, no sign of Sarah and Ethan. As they navigated the dimly lit hallway, a palpable determination enveloped them like a cloak, shielding them from a seemingly world of doubt.

"Max," Lexi began, her voice low and steady. "We need to be meticulous with this plan. One misstep could bring everything crashing down."

"I've got this Lexi. You need to trust me," Max replied, her eyes fixed straight ahead. She flexed her fingers, her thoughts drifting to the potential consequences that loomed large in the shadows.

As they reached the end of the hallway, Max paused for a moment, surveying the empty corridor.

"Lexi," Max said, her voice tinged with concern. "Are you ready for this? I mean, truly ready?"

"Ready as I'll ever be," Lexi admitted with a small smile. "But, Max...the truth is, I'm scared. This whole situation feels like we're walking on a tightrope with no safety net below."

Max reached out and squeezed Lexi's hand reassuringly. "Welcome to war," she said, her own fears mirrored in Lexi's eyes. "But we have to try, right? For Congresswoman Marsh and Will."

The long hallway stretched before them, shadows clinging to the walls like whispered secrets. A fluorescent light flickered overhead, casting an eerie glow on the polished floor tiles.

"Wait," Max whispered, holding up a hand. She cocked her head, listening intently. "Do you hear that?"

A faint sound echoed down the hall, the ghostly residue of a hushed conversation. The campaign headquarters should have been empty this late at night. Max strained to make out the words, but they slipped through her grasp like smoke. "Someone's coming. Hide." Max darted into an alcove, pulling Lexi into her. They held their breath as two figures emerged from around a corner, their faces obscured by shadow.

"Did you tell her?" one asked, his voice low and

insistent.

"Of course not," came the reply, a woman's dulcet tones laced with venom. "She won't know what hit her. I'll meet you at the Hotel Luz tonight to pick up what you owe me."

The pair continued down the hall, their footsteps fading away like echoes of a nightmare. Max exhaled slowly, her heart still hammering against her ribs.

"Was that Jenny?" Lexi asked.

"Sounded like it," Max confirmed, her jaw set in a tight line. "And whoever she's working with."

It was a game of chess, each piece moving in carefully calculated steps. Max knew the stakes were high, but she refused to be a pawn in someone else's twisted game.

They slipped from their hiding place, the shadows swallowing them as they moved in pursuit of their quarry. Max couldn't help but feel the heat of Lexi's presence beside her, a reminder of the promise she'd made to protect her.

"We can't let her get away," Max said, pulling Lexi's hand behind her.

෴෴෴෴

The bustling city expanded before them, the sky painted in shades of orange and crimson. Lexi and Max made their way through the crowded streets, senses heightened by the urgency of their mission.

"Are you sure this is the right place?" Lexi asked, her voice barely audible above the din of traffic and pedestrians. She kept her gaze fixed on the entrance of a sleek, glass-fronted building, its facade reflecting the fiery hues of the sunset.

Max nodded, her eyes narrowing as she scanned the area for any signs of danger. "This is where Jenny said she was to meet her contact tonight. We need to catch her in the act, and if we're lucky we can gather enough evidence to bring down the whole operation without getting our hands dirty."

"Right." Lexi took a deep breath, steeling herself for what was to come. Her heart pounded in her chest, a potent mix of adrenaline and fear coursing through her veins.

The pair waited, concealed by the shadows, eyes never straying from the illuminated entrance. Time seemed to slow to a crawl, each minute stretching out like an eternity. Lexi tried to focus on the task at hand, but the tight confines had Max's body pressing against hers.

"Lexi!" Max's whispered warning jolted her back to the present. Her eyes snapped to the building entrance just in time to see Jenny slipping inside, her figure barely visible through the throngs of people.

"Let's go."

As they cautiously navigated the maze of hallways inside the building, Lexi couldn't help but feel the reality of the situation bearing down on her. The lives and reputations of those she cared about hung in the balance, and one false move could bring everything crashing down.

"Wait." Max suddenly halted, her hand gripping Lexi's arm as they peered around a corner. There, at the end of the dimly lit corridor, stood Jenny, engaged in a hushed conversation with a man whose face was obscured by shadow.

"Is that him? Is that Brown?" Lexi asked, her heart pounding in her ears.

"Looks like it." Max's voice was tense, her fingers tightening around her phone. "We need to get closer. Record their conversation."

"Got it." Lexi nodded, swallowing the lump of fear that had lodged itself in her throat. They crept closer, every step precise, her breath shallow and controlled.

As they neared the pair, Lexi could make out snippets of their heated exchange. "...the congresswoman must never find out..." The words sent a chill down her spine, her pulse quickening as the danger became all too real.

"Almost there," Max whispered, her eyes locked on their target. But just as she raised the cell phone, a sudden noise echoed through the corridor—the sharp click of a high heel against the polished floor.

"Did you hear that?" Jenny said, searching the darkness.

"No, you're being paranoid. No one knows about this place. Here, take this and give it to Horton. He'll know what to do next."

"Are you sure?" Jenny's voice lowered.

"It's all set. You just get Will to the room at the event, and we'll do the rest."

Lexi looked at Max. Max raised a finger to her lips and motioned back the way they came. It was time to get the hell out of there before they were discovered.

Chapter Fourteen

The soft chime of the café's doorbell announced Lexi's arrival, pulling Max's gaze from her steaming cup of coffee. A warm smile spread across her face as she spotted Lexi weaving through the small tables, her gait filled   with determination. The quiet hum of conversation provided a comforting backdrop as Lexi slid into the vacant seat across from Max. Their shoulders brushed briefly, and a sudden jolt of electricity passed between them.

"Hey, Max," Lexi said, her voice hushed but warm. "Thanks for meeting me here. I thought we could use a break from all the cloak-and-dagger stuff. Well, I could use a break," she confessed.

"Of course," Max replied, her eyes revealing a hint of curiosity.

A petite waitress approached their table, her apron adorned with colorful patches. Lexi ordered a cappuccino while Max decided on a refill of her black coffee. As they waited for their drinks, Lexi took a deep breath, her fingers tapping nervously on the wooden table.

"Max," she began, her voice slightly hesitant. "I've been meaning to ask you about your time in the army. You don't talk about it much, and I can't help but be curious."

Max shifted in her seat, her eyes momentarily darting toward the window before settling back on Lexi. She hesitated, weighing the decision to reveal more of her past.

"It's not something I usually share," Max said with a small nod.

Their eyes locked, and the world around them seemed to fall away. As if drawn by an invisible force, their faces inched closer, their breaths mingling with the steam from their coffee cups. The moment was charged with anticipation, yet Max did not want to break the spell by looking away.

Max took a deep breath, steeling herself to share more about her time in the army. "I was part of a special operations unit," she began, her voice measured and steady. "We were tasked with high-risk missions, often involving intelligence gathering, hostage rescue, and counterterrorism."

"Wow," Lexi breathed out, leaning forward as if to absorb every word. "That must have been intense."

"Intense is an understatement," Max replied with a wry smile. "The training alone was brutal, endless hours of physical conditioning, weapons training, and learning how to think on my feet. There were times I thought I wouldn't make it." She paused, remembering the grueling exercises that had pushed her body to its limits.

"Sounds like you gained some valuable skills, though," Lexi observed, her eyes filled with admiration.

"Definitely," Max agreed, a hint of pride coloring her tone. "But it wasn't just the tactical abilities that were important. I also learned a lot about teamwork, trust, and leadership—things that have carried over into my current career."

"Color me impressed," Lexi said. "It's part of why I'm so passionate about politics. I want to create a better world for people who put their lives on the line for others."

"Tell me more about your political aspirations," Max said, genuinely curious about Lexi's goals and motivations.

"Ever since I was young, I knew I wanted to be involved in shaping our country's future," Lexi divulged, her eyes shining with enthusiasm. "I started by volunteering on local campaigns, then worked my way up to become Congresswoman Marsh's campaign manager. I've seen firsthand how good policies can improve lives, and I want to be a part of that change."

"Sounds like you're committed to making a difference," Max said.

"Absolutely," Lexi replied, her enthusiasm unwavering. "And I'm not going to let anything, or anyone, stand in the way of progress."

As their conversation deepened, Max found herself both captivated and challenged by Lexi's passion for politics.

They leaned toward one another, their bodies drawn like magnets, as if pulled by an invisible force. The café seemed to fade away, leaving only the two of them locked in this moment. Their eyes met, lingering on each other as the air crackled with electricity.

Max traced the rim of her coffee cup with her fingertip, gathering the courage to delve into a more personal part of her past. The dimly lit café seemed to embrace them, providing a sense of security that allowed her to lower her guard.

"Lexi," she began hesitantly. "There's something I haven't told many people, something from my time in the army." She took a deep breath, her eyes searching Lexi's for understanding. "I lost someone very close to me during combat. It was...it was the hardest thing I've ever had to deal with."

Lexi tentatively reached across the table, her fingers gently brushing Max's hand in a gesture of support. "I'm so sorry, Max. I can't imagine what that must have been like for you."

A ghost of a smile flickered across Max's face as memories of Sergeant Tony Micheals filled her mind. "He was like a brother to me. We went through everything together—basic training, deployments, you name it. Losing him left a hole in my heart that's never quite healed."

"I am so sorry," Lexi murmured, her voice soft and full of empathy as she covered Max's hand with her own. She paused, her expression thoughtful. "When I was younger, my family struggled financially, and for a while, we were even homeless. That experience shaped me into who I am today, and it's a big reason why I'm so dedicated to fighting for better policies. It's nothing compared to what you went through, but I think our journeys are what make us who we are."

Max smiled and squeezed Lexi's hand. "I agree."

Max leaned back in her chair, the warm sunlight filtering through the café windows casting patterns on her face. She glanced around the quiet room before returning her gaze to Lexi, who was sipping her coffee with a thoughtful expression.

"Lexi, there's something I've been worried about," Max began, her voice low and urgent. "Jenny is Will's girlfriend and her meal ticket to a better future. I'm concerned she might spill her involvement in the blackmail plot to Will in order to protect herself and get him on her side."

Lexi furrowed her brow, taking in Max's words. "I see your point, but why would she do that?"

"Desperation, maybe? Fear?" Max sighed. "I can't be sure, but we need to stay one step ahead of her if we want to keep Will safe and expose the truth."

As they discussed the situation, Max's mind drifted back to her time in the army, where she'd often faced high-stakes situations that required quick thinking and decisive action. She remembered the grit of sand beneath her boots as she navigated foreign terrain, the heft of her rifle in her hands, and the concern of what they were doing resting firmly on her fellow soldiers' shoulders.

"Max, if you're right," Lexi agreed, snapping Max back to the present moment. "We need to make sure Jenny doesn't undermine our efforts. But how?"

As they plotted their next steps, Max couldn't help but think back to when she first met Lexi—the fiery passion for justice that burned in her eyes, the intelligence and determination that radiated from her every word.

"Max," Lexi murmured, reaching across the table to grasp her hand. "Whatever happens, I want you to know that I'm with you every step of the way."

"Thank you, Lexi," Max replied, feeling a swell of emotion at the sincere declaration.

As they left the café, Max felt an unfamiliar sense of vulnerability mixed with strength—a potent combination for someone like Max who wasn't used to talking about herself.

Max's concern about Jenny's possible betrayal weighed heavily on her mind as she paced the small hotel suite, her steps echoing in the silence. Lexi sat at the kitchen table, her fingers drumming a nervous rhythm against the wooden surface. She watched Max's movements, perhaps sensing the tension radiating from her.

"Max," Lexi called out softly, trying to catch her gaze. "You need to sit down and relax. We'll figure this out."

Finally stopping, Max turned toward Lexi and took a deep breath. With a nod, she pulled out a chair and joined Lexi at the table, their eyes meeting in a silent exchange of support. Lexi reached out, gently placing her hand on Max's forearm, offering comfort.

"Tell me what's going through your head right now," Lexi urged, her voice soothing and calm.

Max hesitated for a moment before speaking. "I just can't shake the feeling that Jenny might try to save herself by blaming someone else. She could easily tell Will everything and make it look like we're the bad guys."

As the conversation shifted to planning their next move, a sudden knock on the door startled them both. Their eyes locked, fear and uncertainty flashing between them.

"Who could that be?" Lexi whispered, her grip on Max's hand tightening.

Max shook her head, her pulse quickening as she rose from her chair and approached the door. The peephole revealed a figure standing outside, their features obscured by the dim hallway lighting. Drawing upon her training and instincts, Max took a deep breath, ready to confront the unexpected visitor.

"Stay behind me," she instructed Lexi, her voice low and steady.

With her heart pounding in her ears, Max opened the door just enough to reveal the person standing on the other side. As the tension in the room reached its peak, the identity of their visitor became clear.

"Hello, ladies," the familiar voice greeted them, an ominous undertone lurking beneath the surface. "We need to talk." Sam walked through the door. "We might have a problem. I'm worried about the event tomorrow night."

Chapter Fifteen

The high-dollar campaign event buzzed with excitement, the opulent ballroom bathed in a warm golden light. Crystal chandeliers hung from the ceiling, casting intricate shadows on the guests below. Lexi stood near the edge of the dance floor, her eyes scanning the room as she took in the luxurious surroundings. She felt the seriousness of the evening's importance press down on her, but she was determined not to show it.

"Come on, Max!" Lexi called out over the din of conversation and laughter. She grabbed Max's hand, her eyes radiant with mischief. "Let's dance. We'll blend in. As you wheel me around the dance floor, we can see things better."

Max hesitated for a moment, but Lexi tugged her onto the parquet floor, insistent, and teased a smile from Max's lips. The music swelled around them, the sultry notes of a jazz band weaving through the air like a spell.

"Watch my back, will you?" Lexi whispered into Max's ear.

"Always," Max replied, her head on a swivel as they began to dance. Her body moved effortlessly to the rhythm despite her constant vigilance. Lexi admired her grace and confidence, knowing that beneath the elegant facade, Max was a force to be reckoned with.

As they twirled around the dance floor, Lexi caught glimpses of Hank and Jules mingling among the crowd. Max's team blended in seamlessly, sipping champagne and exchanging pleasantries while keeping a keen eye on their surroundings. Lexi knew they were searching for any potential threats, and the knowledge both comforted and reminded her of why they were there. She also knew that Max was wound tight as a drum.

"Relax, Max," Lexi murmured. "You've got this under control."

❧❧❧❧

Max nodded, trying to push away her worries and focus on the present. The music enveloped her, the rich melodies resonating deep within her chest. She let herself be swept up in the dance, her body moving in perfect harmony with Lexi's.

"Enjoying yourself?" Lexi asked, a playful smile tugging at the corners of her lips.

"Actually, yes," Max admitted, warmth blossoming in her chest. "This is exactly what I needed."

"Good," Lexi said, satisfaction evident in her voice. "You deserve a little fun, you know."

As they continued to dance, Max allowed herself to get lost in the moment, in the sound of laughter and the clink of champagne glasses. For a few brief minutes, she could forget about the pressure of the campaign, the looming threat of blackmail, and the knowledge that there were dangerous forces at work against them.

But even as she reveled in the romance and glamour of the evening, a small part of her couldn't help but remain on high alert, her senses attuned to any sign of danger lurking just beneath the surface. The night was only just beginning, and she knew that anything could happen before it was over.

The music and laughter faded into the background as Max's radio crackled to life. "Max, we've got a disturbance on the lawn. Need you out here ASAP."

"Copy that," Max replied, her heart rate spiking. She turned to Lexi, her eyes urgent. "I have to go. Stay here, and stay vigilant."

"Be careful," Lexi murmured, concern etched on her face.

"Always." Max reassured her with a quick smile before disappearing into the crowd.

Outside on the lawn, Max assessed the disturbance—a heated argument between two guests—and quickly defused the situation. The altercation was so ridiculous that Max initially thought it had been fabricated, but these were elite movers and shakers, and in her short time with the congresswoman she'd learned that the political class had a way of turning any small action into absurdly high drama. Still, her instincts told her this was more than a mere coincidence, and she hurried back inside, her senses heightened.

≈≈≈≈

Left alone, Lexi surveyed the room, her pulse thrumming with unease. The opulent chandeliers cast flickering shadows on the walls, making it difficult to discern anything amiss. But she couldn't shake the feeling that something was wrong.

"Hey there." Jenny approached Lexi, a flirty smile playing on her lips. "Will and I thought you might like a drink to calm your nerves." She held out a champagne flute filled with bubbling liquid.

"Thanks," Lexi said hesitantly, taking the glass.

She rarely drank, but the tension in the air was getting to her. As she sipped the champagne, a strange sensation washed over her—a wave of dizziness and disorientation.

"Are you okay?" Jenny asked with what sounded like exaggerated concern. "You don't look so good. Maybe you should freshen up in the bathroom. I'll come with you."

"Maybe you're right," Lexi mumbled, her voice distant and slurred. She placed a hand on Jenny's arm for support as they made their way through the crowd.

In the dimly lit bathroom, Lexi leaned against the cold marble counter, trying to clear her head. But the disorientation only intensified, and as she glanced at her reflection in the mirror, her vision blurred.

"Here," Jenny said, handing her a damp cloth. "This should help."

"Thanks," Lexi whispered, feeling vulnerable and exposed. She pressed the cloth to her face, but it provided little relief. Her legs began to buckle beneath her.

"Let me help you," Jenny offered, wrapping an arm around Lexi's waist. Her voice was soothing, but her eyes were cold and calculating.

Something isn't right, Lexi thought, her mind struggling to piece together what was happening. But her thoughts were sluggish, tangled in a fog of confusion and fear.

As Jenny led Lexi out of the bathroom and down a dimly lit corridor, Lexi's last coherent thought was of Max—the way her eyes had sparkled on the dance floor, the strength and warmth of her embrace. A desperate plea for help formed in her mind, but the darkness closed in, swallowing her whole.

A cold, metallic floor pressed against Lexi's cheek as she stirred back to consciousness. The darkness was all-consuming, broken only by her shallow, labored breaths. She tried to lift her head, but a wave of nausea crashed over her, sending her back down into the icy embrace of the metal floor.

"Lexi?" Will's voice came from somewhere close, but the blackness and the echo reverberating made it impossible to tell exactly where. "Is that you? I can't see anything. What's going on?"

"I don't know," Lexi admitted, her thoughts still muddled and sluggish. She pushed herself up, using her hands to brace her weight, and immediately regretted it. Pain throbbed behind her eyes, and she clenched her teeth to keep from crying out.

"Where are we?" Will asked, his voice tinged with panic.

The smell of old oil, wood, and rust assaulted her senses. "It echoes like all the walls are metal. And it's big...I can't touch anything in any direction from here. Maybe, like, a shipping container?" As she spoke, the frigid air stung her lungs, its icy tendrils wrapping around her heart and ramping up her own fear.

"Can you stand?" Will's voice sounded closer now, and she reached out, her fingers brushing against something solid—his arm. They clung to each other for reassurance.

"Let's try," Lexi said, finding her footing as she rose unsteadily. The cramped space allowed for little movement, and she stretched her arms out, searching for walls or any sign of an exit.

"Damn it, we're trapped," Will muttered, his voice strained. "What do they want with us?"

"Whoever they are, they wanted to get us out of that event," Lexi reasoned, her mind working overtime to make sense of their predicament. "We need to find a way out of here."

Think, Lexi, think, she told herself, her heart pounding in her chest. *What would Max do?*

"Help me look for a weak spot," she instructed Will, her voice more confident than she felt. Together, they explored the confines of their metal prison, feeling along the walls and floor for any hidden openings or weaknesses.

But as the minutes stretched on, hopelessness set in. There was no way out—at least, not one that they could see or feel.

"Lexi," Will whispered, his voice breaking. "I'm scared."

"Me too," she admitted, swallowing hard. She thought of Max again, how safe she'd felt in her arms. But now, more than ever, she needed to be strong for both Will and herself.

"Hey," she said softly, her hand finding Will's in the darkness. "We're going to get through this. We just need to keep our heads and stay focused."

"Right," he said, squeezing her fingers tightly. With their fear and desperation drawing them closer, they continued to search for a way out even as the darkness threatened to swallow them whole.

Despite their efforts, the oppressive blackness remained unyielding, as if it were a living entity determined to hold them captive. The cold metal walls seemed to close in on them with every passing minute, amplifying Lexi's claustrophobia.

"Is there anything? Anything at all?" Will asked, his breath shallow as he frantically searched for any possible exit.

"Nothing yet," Lexi replied, her voice strained from the mounting dread she couldn't ignore. She felt the walls and floor again, fingers tracing over the rough surface, praying for an imperfection that could lead to their escape.

"Damn it!" Will shouted, pounding his fist against the wall. "Why can't we find a way out?"

"Stay calm, Will. Panic won't help us," Lexi advised, though she, too, was struggling with her own rising panic. Her thoughts turned to Max, wondering if she had noticed their absence yet or if she was still caught up in the chaos outside.

"Let's try this again," Lexi suggested, forcing her trembling hands to steady themselves. "We have to be methodical. Start in one corner and work our way around."

"Okay," Will agreed, his voice quivering. He began anew, systematically searching every inch of their confined space.

"What about the ceiling?" Lexi thought aloud. Her eyes strained against the darkness, desperate to make out any signs of a trapdoor or weak spot above them.

"Nothing. It's just as solid as the rest of this hellhole," Will said despairingly.

"Keep looking, Will. We can't give up," Lexi urged, her heart racing in her chest. She knew they were running out of time, but she refused to let herself think about what would happen if they didn't find a way out.

"Lexi, I..." Will hesitated, his fear evident in the

tremor of his voice. "If we don't make it out of here, I just want you to know that I'm sorry for everything. For the mess I've gotten us both into."

"Hey, you didn't do this," Lexi said, her hand finding his again in the darkness. "We're not giving up yet. We still have each other, right?"

"Right." Will seemed somewhat reassured by Lexi's determination, although Lexi didn't feel very sure.

"Then let's keep going," she said, her voice resolute. She continued searching, a silent prayer echoing through her brain as she looked for any sign of hope within the metal tomb that held them captive.

The minutes dragged on, and with every failed attempt to find an escape, her desperation grew. Their once-methodical approach gave way to frenzied scrambling, hands grasping at anything that might lead to freedom.

"Please," Lexi whispered, her voice breaking as reality began to sink in. There was no visible exit, no weakness to exploit. The crushing feelings of helplessness threatened to consume her, but she knew she couldn't give up, not while there was still breath in her lungs.

"Let's try one more time," Lexi suggested, her voice wavering but determined.

Lexi's heart hammered in her chest, the sound echoing loudly in her ears, almost drowning out Will's rapid breathing beside her. The air inside the shipping container was thick with a musty desperation, a stifling reminder of their dire circumstances.

"Wait," Will whispered suddenly, halting his frantic search. "Do you hear that?"

Lexi strained her ears, trying to pick up on

whatever had caught Will's attention. And then she heard it too—a faint electronic humming that seemed to emanate from one corner of their prison.

"Is that..." Lexi trailed off, not wanting to voice what they both feared.

"Let's find out," Will said grimly, making his way toward the sound.

As they approached the source of the noise, Lexi's heart raced as a small, slow-blinking red light came into view. When she got close enough, she thought she could make out a small camera mounted near the ceiling, accompanied by a speaker.

"Shit," Will muttered under his breath. "They've been watching us this whole time."

"Hello, Lexi and Will," a distorted voice crackled through the speaker, sending chills down Lexi's spine. She couldn't be certain, but she thought she recognized the voice as belonging to Tom Horton, the counterterrorism expert turned blackmailer.

"Tom," Lexi spat, clenching her fists. "You won't get away with this. People will find us."

"Ah, but Lexi," Tom replied mockingly. "That's where you're wrong. No one even knows you're missing yet. By the time they start to suspect anything, it'll be far too late."

"Please," Will interjected, his voice pleading. "My mother doesn't deserve this. None of us do."

"Your mother made her choice when she decided to run for office," Tom retorted coldly. "And now, you both will pay the price."

"Let us go, Tom," Lexi said, her voice wavering but determined. "We can figure something out, a deal, anything. Just let us go."

"Sorry, Lexi," Tom replied, his tone devoid of all

emotion. "There's no negotiating here. Enjoy your stay."

The speaker fell silent, leaving only the sound of their own ragged breaths to fill the void. Lexi felt hot tears well up in her eyes as the burden of their situation settled upon her like a leaden jacket.

"Come here," Will whispered, pulling Lexi into a tight embrace. Their bodies trembled against each other from fear and the biting cold of the container, made worse by the uncertainty as they faced the unknown.

"Will," Lexi murmured into his chest. "I'm scared."

"Me too, Lexi," he admitted, his voice raw with emotion. "But we'll find a way out of this. We have to."

As they clung to one another in the oppressive darkness, Lexi could feel the faintest flicker of hope rekindling within her. They had been dealt a terrible hand, but she refused to give up. Together, they would face whatever horrors awaited them. And maybe, just maybe, they would find a way to survive.

The dim glow of the camera's red light pulsed agonizingly slowly, injecting a sinister energy into the stale air. Lexi's heart raced in tandem with Will's shallow breaths as they huddled together, their gazes locked onto the unblinking eye that watched their every move.

"Ah, there you are." Jose Guevara's accent oozed through the speaker, smooth and malevolent. "You two must be getting quite cozy in there. It's good to see you again, Will."

Lexi felt Will cringe when he heard the voice. "Do you know him?"

She felt him nod. "I think he was my drug dealer in college."

"Fuck me. It all makes sense now. That's how

they are blackmailing your mother. Shit." Lexi felt like she was going to be sick. How could she have been so stupid?

She started to put the pieces of the puzzle together, Jenny, Dan, the meeting at the hotel. Of course Jenny knew about Will's college days. She was there for the whole scandal.

Bitch.

"Please," Lexi pleaded, her voice shaking. "We don't know what you want, but we can work something out. Just let us go."

"Work something out?" Dan Brown sneered, joining the conversation. "Your naivety is almost endearing, Ms. Anders. But this isn't some business deal we can negotiate."

"Will," Tom interjected, his icy tone sending shivers down Lexi's spine. "Your mother has made quite a few enemies in her time. We're here to settle the score." His words hung in the air, thick with menace.

"Is it money you want?" Will asked, desperation evident in his wavering voice. "My family has money. I'm sure we can—"

"Money?" Dan cut him off, laughing darkly. "No, no, my dear boy. This is about so much more than mere money."

"Then what do you want?" Lexi demanded, anger rising within her like a boiling pot. "Why have you taken us?"

"Perhaps it's the thrill of the game," Jose mused, his voice dripping with malice. "Or maybe we just want to see that esteemed congresswoman fall from grace."

"Whatever it is," Lexi said, her eyes narrowing with resolve, "we'll fight it. You won't break us."

"Bold words, Ms. Anders," Tom replied, his voice

chillingly devoid of emotion. "But we'll see how long that bravado lasts."

"Tom, please," Will said, his voice cracking under the weight of his emotions. "You don't have to do this. We can work something out. Just let us go."

"Sorry, Will," Tom responded coldly. "No deals, no negotiations. You're just collateral damage in a much larger game."

With that, the speaker fell silent, leaving Lexi and Will to stew in their own fear and uncertainty. As they clung together in the oppressive darkness, Lexi felt an odd mixture of despair and determination settle in her chest. She refused to give up, knowing that their survival depended on it.

"Will," she whispered, her voice heavy with emotion. "We'll find a way out of this. We have to."

"Lexi," he murmured back, his breath warm against her ear. "I'm not so sure. How did this happen?"

Lexi knew Will had a right to know about Jenny, but should she be the one to tell him? Was now the time? He deserved to know that his girlfriend was the reason he was sitting here right now. She'd helped set him up and lured Lexi to the bathroom to kidnap her.

Lexi reached for his hands and whispered, "Will, I'm afraid I have some bad news."

"Wh-what is it?"

She searched his face and tried to swallow the lump in her throat. "Jenny is helping the people who kidnapped us."

"What? That can't be possible."

"I know it's hard to believe, but we found out when we started investigating the blackmail plot against your mother."

"My mom? Mom is being blackmailed? When?

Who? Why am I just...I can't believe this. How...."

"I know this is a lot to unpack, Will. Let's focus on getting out of here." Lexi looked over her shoulder at the camera, then back at Will. "Once we're out of here, I'll tell you everything and show you the evidence. I don't want you to get blindsided when this goes exposed."

Will dropped his head into his hands, his body wracked with sobs. "I sure know how to pick them, don't I? My poor mom. She bailed me out of the whole drug-dealing stuff, putting herself at risk, and now this. I'm so sorry Lexi. I really am."

Lexi hugged his shoulder and gently rocked him. "We're going to get through this, don't worry. I know Max will find us and rescue us."

Lexi's heart pounded in her chest, each beat like a staccato drum echoing through the cramped confines of the container. She could feel Will trembling beside her, his breath shuddering with every exhale. The cold metal walls seemed to close in on them, offering no solace or reprieve from their desperate situation.

Will seemed to get himself together as his crying stopped and was replaced with steadier breathing. Lexi could feel a shift in his energy, and when he lifted his head from her shoulder, it was clear that desperation and anger had replaced despair. He puffed his chest and yelled, turning toward the camera. "Please! We've never done anything to hurt you. Why are you doing this?"

There was no response from their captors, only the unsettling silence that had become all too familiar. Lexi's mind raced, searching for some way—any way—to break free from this prison. But even as her thoughts tumbled over one another, she couldn't escape the growing realization that they were at the mercy of strangers.

"Dammit," she hissed under her breath, her frustration mounting.

"Maybe that's all we are to them, pawns in getting to my mother," Will said, his voice barely audible. "But we can't let them win, Lexi. We can't give up."

As if on cue, the speaker crackled to life, and the cold, detached voice of their tormentor filled the air once more. "Just remember, you two," Tom sneered. "Every second that ticks by brings you closer to your fate. It's only a matter of time before we decide what that will be."

"Go to hell!" Lexi shouted, her anger flaring. "You won't break us! Do you hear me? You won't!"

"Lexi," Will murmured, reaching out to grab her hand.

"It's okay. I'm sure Max has realized something's happened. She'll get here. I'm sure of it," she whispered. She didn't want their captors to hear her. At least she hoped that Max had realized by now they were nowhere to be found.

She took a deep breath to try to steady her racing heart. As they huddled together in the darkness, Lexi could feel the warmth of Will's body against her own, a small comfort amid the cold and despair. Their fear and desperation seemed to draw them closer, an unspoken bond forming in the face of terror.

"Will," Lexi whispered, her voice thick with emotion. "No matter what happens, I want you to know that I'm grateful for you."

"Grateful?" he asked, voice full of confusion.

"Yeah," she said, allowing a sad smile to form on her lips. "For being here with me. For not giving up. For reminding me that we're not alone."

"Lexi, I wouldn't want to face this with anyone else."

As they clung to one another, the darkness around them somehow seemed a little less oppressive, the cold a little less chilling. Though they were still at the mercy of their captors, they had each other, and in that moment, it was enough to keep hope alive.

"Hey," Lexi muttered, trying to inject some bravado into her voice. "We can't just sit here and wait for them to make their next move."

"Right," Will agreed, his voice strained with fear. "But what can we do?"

Lexi scanned their bleak surroundings, her eyes fully adjusted to the darkness. Her gaze fell upon a faint glimmer at the edge of the container. A small   rip in the metal, barely noticeable before.

"Will, look," she whispered, her voice trembling with cautious excitement. "There's a rip in the corner!"

"Are you sure?" he asked.

"Positive," Lexi confirmed, her heart pounding in her chest. "Maybe...maybe we can use it to our advantage."

With renewed determination, they scrambled across the cold metal floor, hands searching for anything that could be used as a tool. Lexi's fingers closed around a discarded screwdriver—a stroke of luck in their otherwise dismal circumstances.

"Here," she said, handing the tool to Will. "Try to pry open the rip."

As he wedged the screwdriver into the gap, Lexi held her breath. The metal groaned in protest, but after several tense moments, the opening widened ever so slightly.

"Keep going," Lexi urged, her voice barely above a whisper, afraid to alert their captors. "We can do this."

"Damn, it's tough."

"Here, let me help," Lexi said, positioning herself beside him, her fear momentarily eclipsed by the hope of escape.

The two worked in tandem, their efforts fueled by desperation. Each inch they pried open felt like a small victory, a testament to their resolve. Their hands were raw and bloody, but neither gave any thought to the pain—the promise of freedom was too alluring.

"Lexi." Will panted, pausing for a moment to catch his breath. "If we make it out of here, I want you to know that anything you need, you just ask."

"Thanks," Lexi whispered, touched by his admission.

As the gap widened, so too did the fragile flame of hope flickering within them. Perhaps, against all odds, they might just stand a chance.

With every groan of the metal, every bead of sweat dripping from her brow, Lexi felt the gravity of their situation pressing down on them. The sliver of hope they'd found in the hidden rip seemed to grow more precarious with each passing second.

"Come on," Lexi muttered through gritted teeth, her fingers aching as she clutched at the makeshift tool. "We're so close."

"Damn it," Will hissed, frustration lacing his voice as he struggled to pry open the compartment. "I can't get enough leverage."

"Here," Lexi said, adjusting her position to give him more room. "Try now."

The sound of straining metal filled the container, punctuated by their labored breaths. Time seemed to stretch out before them, each minute an eternity as they fought for their lives.

"Lexi," Will whispered suddenly. "Do you hear that?"

She strained her ears, trying to pick up on what had caught his attention. And then she heard it too—footsteps, growing closer by the second.

"Quick!" she said, her heart pounding in her chest. "We have to hurry!"

As if spurred on by the imminent threat, they doubled their efforts, their movements frantic and desperate. The gap in the metal widened just enough for Will to slip his fingers through it, pulling with all his might.

"Almost there!" he cried. "Just a little more."

"Please, please, please," Lexi chanted under her breath, her entire world narrowing down to the stubborn piece of metal that stood between them and freedom.

Time was running out. The footsteps grew louder, echoing ominously through the darkness. Lexi's pulse roared in her ears, drowning out all else as fear threatened to consume her.

"Come on, Will," she whispered, her voice choked with emotion. "We can do this. We have to."

Suddenly, the container door swung open, revealing a blinding light that pierced the darkness. Lexi and Will squinted against the glare, shielding their eyes as they finally faced the terror that awaited them just beyond the confines of their prison.

"Looks like you two were up to something," a man said, his voice dripping with menace. "But it's too late now."

Lexi's heart sank, a cold dread settling over her as

she realized their hopes of escape had been dashed in an instant. She exchanged a desperate glance with Will, knowing that whatever happened next, they would face it together.

☙☙☙☙

The moonlight danced with the shadows as Lexi and Will were practically dragged across the cold, damp dirt. Lexi's heart raced, each beat echoing in her ears like a ticking clock. Time was running out, and she couldn't help but think of Max and the others frantically searching for them. At least, she hoped they were.

"Keep moving," one of their captors barked, tightening his grip on Lexi's arm. She winced but refused to let him see her pain.

Will stumbled beside her, his face a mask of defiance. Despite their fear, they drew strength from each other, their unwavering gazes communicating a silent vow: they would not give in without a fight.

"Where are you taking us?" Lexi demanded, her voice steady and strong despite the terror that clenched her insides. The man dragging her only chuckled darkly, offering no answers.

As they approached an old, crumbling building, Lexi felt her chest tighten. The structure loomed over them like a predatory beast, and she knew instinctively that whatever awaited them inside would be far worse than what they had already endured.

"Inside," the second man ordered, shoving Will forward. Lexi caught Will's eye for a moment, holding the connection between them as if it were a lifeline. She saw his determination, his refusal to cower before their enemies. It fueled her own resolve, giving her the strength to face the darkness within.

They were led down a narrow, dimly lit corridor, the guards' heavy footsteps echoing ominously around them. Lexi strained her senses, trying to pick up any clues that might help them escape. But all she could hear was her own ragged breathing, the pounding of her heart, and the faint, sinister whispers of their captors.

"Here," one of them grunted, stopping before a solid metal door. It opened with a screech, revealing a room that smelled of damp and decay. Lexi's stomach churned, but she set her jaw and stepped inside, refusing to show weakness.

"Sit," the other one ordered, gesturing to two rickety chairs in the center of the room. Lexi and Will exchanged a glance before reluctantly obeying. They were quickly bound to the chairs and the two men left the room.

"Good," the first man said as he locked the door behind them. "Now we wait."

Lexi glanced at Will, her mind racing with desperate plans and half-formed ideas. She needed to find a way to get them out of this nightmare, to save not only herself but also the man beside her who had become an unwitting victim in this twisted game.

"Will," she whispered, her voice barely audible over the sound of her pounding heart. "We can't just sit here and do nothing. We have to find a way out."

He nodded, his eyes filled with grim determination. "I know. But what can we do?"

"Anything," Lexi replied, her desperation giving way to a steely resolve. "Everything. I won't let them win, Will. I won't let them break us."

As they sat in the oppressive darkness, their captors' laughter echoing through the halls like the howls of wolves, Lexi and Will clung to each other, their fear and determination forging a bond that could not be broken. And as they tried to plot their escape, the flicker of hope that had been ignited in their hearts was slowly extinguishing.

"Are you comfortable?" A chillingly familiar voice crackled over a speaker, causing both Lexi and Will to freeze. "Do you really think we'd leave such an obvious way out of that container? Silly kids."

Lexi didn't recognize this voice. It was different, more evil. "Who the fuck are you?" Lexi demanded, her voice shaking with anger and fear. "You'll never get away with this. Just wait till I get my hands on you. I'm going to fucking kill you."

"Really?" the voice taunted. "We'll see how long your bravery lasts, Ms. Anders."

"Let Will go," Lexi snarled, her protective instincts flaring. "This is between you and me."

"Is it?" The voice sounded almost amused. "Interesting perspective, considering he's here because of you. You think we didn't know about your little plan to expose us?"

"Enough!" Lexi shouted, her frustration boiling over. "Just tell us what you want!"

"Perhaps we can make a deal," the voice mused, sounding as though they were considering their options. "Give us what we want, and we might just let you go."

"Which is?" Lexi asked cautiously, her heart pounding in her chest.

"Congresswoman Marsh's resignation," the voice replied, the words dripping with venom. "And then we'll discuss your release."

"Go to hell," she spat, trying to think of anything she could say to gain any type of advantage. "We didn't just plan to expose you, we called the FBI and they were surveilling the event. It's just a matter of time before they come breaking down your door."

Chapter Sixteen

Max searched the area, frantically looking for Lexi, Will, and Jenny.

Nothing.

A large, bulky envelope with Congresswoman Marsh's name on it had been found at the front of the hall. Max grabbed it by the corner and located Congresswoman Marsh, who was frantic now.

"Where are they?" she demanded. "This wasn't part of the fucking plan, Max. Bring them back. I don't care what it takes. I'll abandon my campaign, I'll do anything, but get them back right now. I can't believe I agreed to this."

"Congresswoman, remain calm. We don't want anyone suspecting anything," Max said, looking at the vibrating room, the guests dancing, drinking, and enjoying the campaign event, oblivious that anything was amiss. "Sam, we need a quiet extraction. Bring the car around front and wait for us."

"You got it," Sam replied through her earpiece.

"Hank, Jules, maintain surveillance of the event and let me know who leaves or has left suddenly."

"You got it, boss."

Everyone was calm and reserved as the team took up their positions at the event. Max took the congresswoman's elbow and quickly guided her to the waiting car.

Max stood in Congresswoman Marsh's office, her heart pounding as the congresswoman inserted the CD into the player. The two women exchanged a tense glance before turning their attention to the television.

"Listen closely," the distorted voice on the recording   began, accompanied by an image of Lexi and Will, both bound and gagged. "If you want to see your campaign manager and son alive again, Congresswoman Marsh, you'll drop out of the race immediately."

Congresswoman Marsh clenched her fists, her face pale with worry. Max's throat tightened at the sight of Lexi helpless and frightened. Her determination to save her surged like a tidal wave, drowning any doubts or fears she may have had.

"We need to find them," Congresswoman Marsh commanded, her voice laced with urgency. "Before it's too late."

Max nodded and turned to Sam "We've got a lead on Lexi and Will's location. Can you use the tracker on Lexi's phone to pinpoint their whereabouts?"

"Give me a minute," Sam replied. His fingers tapped furiously on his keyboard. Max could hear the tension in his voice, reflecting her own anxiety.

While they waited, Congresswoman Marsh paced back and forth, her eyes never leaving the screen displaying the captive pair. "We have to get them, Max," she whispered, the motherly fear evident in her voice.

"I promise, we're going to find them," Max assured her, her voice steady despite the turmoil raging inside her. She couldn't help but feel responsible for Lexi's predicament, and she vowed to bring her back safely—not just for Congresswoman Marsh, but for herself as well.

"Okay, I've got something," Sam said, interrupting Max's thoughts. "I've traced Lexi's phone to an area near the old industrial district. There are a few abandoned warehouses there that could be hiding spots."

"Where are they?" Max asked, her mind already racing with potential plans of action. "We'll assemble a team and check them out."

"Be careful, Max," Sam warned. "There's no telling what kind of dangers await you in those warehouses."

"Oh, you're coming with me, Sam," she replied.

Max turned to Congresswoman Marsh, her eyes steely with resolve. "I'll get the security detail ready. We're going to bring Lexi and Will home."

As they prepared for the rescue mission, Max couldn't help but think of Lexi and her spunky attitude, her intelligence, and the way her eyes seemed to light up whenever they spoke. Whatever it took, Max would make sure that those eyes sparkled once more.

☙ ❧ ❦ ❧

The sun dipped low in the sky, casting eerie shadows over the decaying industrial district. From atop a nearby building, Max surveyed the warehouses below, each one more decrepit than the last. Her heart hammered in her chest as she considered the potential dangers lurking within those crumbling walls.

"Three possible locations," Sam said, joining Max on the rooftop. "Warehouse A has weak security but an unstable structure. Warehouse B is heavily fortified, but there's a hidden entrance through the sewers. And Warehouse C...well, that one's a dark pit."

"Pit or not, we can't afford to overlook any

possibilities," Max replied, her determination unwavering. "We need to cover all our bases."

"Agreed," Sam said, his eyes scanning the area below. "So, who do we have on our team?"

"Jules and Hank from my security detail," Max answered, her mind racing with strategies. "They're both highly skilled and trustworthy."

"Sounds like a solid crew," Sam said. "How do you want to proceed?"

Max didn't answer. Her brain was too busy reflecting on the emotional stakes of this mission—exactly what she had hoped to avoid, but here she was anyway. Not only were Lexi and Will's lives hanging in the balance, but her own heart was at risk as well. The thought of losing Lexi made her chest tighten with anxiety.

"Max," Sam said gently, sensing her inner turmoil. "We'll find them. I promise."

"Thanks, Sam," Max whispered, swallowing hard. "Let's get to work."

⁂

Max studied the blueprints spread across the floor of the tactical van where the team had convened, her fingers tracing the lines that marked potential entry and exit points in each dilapidated warehouse. Her brow furrowed as she tried to anticipate any obstacles or security measures they might encounter.

Going over the plans again, Max said, "Warehouse A has a side entrance that's partially concealed, but it could be booby-trapped," she said, looking up at her team. "Warehouse B's underground entrance is wide open, but there's no cover if we run into trouble."

"Then there's Warehouse C," Sam added, pointing to the third blueprint. "It's got multiple entrances, but the layout inside is like a maze."

"Damn," Jules muttered, frustration evident in her voice. "None of these options are ideal."

"True," Max said, her eyes flicking between the warehouses' layouts. "But we don't have time to wait for ideal. We need to make a decision, and fast."

"Let's break it down from their perspective," Hank said, his typically stoic demeanor betraying a hint of anxiety. "Which one is best for the kidnappers? That's probably where they are."

"Given what we know about these bastards, I'd say Warehouse C," Max replied, gut instinct driving her decision. "They'll want to keep Lexi and Will secure, which means a more complex layout works in their favor."

"Agreed." Sam nodded. "It's risky, but it's our best bet."

"Okay, so let's get to work," Max said, her voice steady despite the pounding of her heart. "We need to assign roles and tasks for everyone.

"Jules, you'll be our point person, making sure we're not walking into any traps. Hank, you're on rear guard, watching our backs. Sam, you and I will focus on finding Lexi and Will."

"Got it, boss," Jules replied, determination shining in her eyes.

"Everyone clear on their responsibilities?" Max asked, scanning the faces around her as they nodded in unison. "Good. Let's gear up, then reconvene for a final briefing."

Max watched her team gather the necessary equipment and supplies, each person focused and determined. They collected communication devices, flashlights, specialized tools, and other essentials for the mission. As she observed them, Max felt a deep sense of responsibility for these people—her friends, her colleagues, her allies in this fight.

"Alright, everyone," Max called out, catching their attention. "Gather around."

As they formed a tight circle, Max glanced at each of them in turn, her eyes serious but reassuring. She knew that the next few hours would test their limits, but she believed in her team.

"We all know that this rescue mission is going to be tough. We're going up against dangerous criminals who won't hesitate to hurt Lexi and Will, or any of us if we give them the chance."

She paused, taking a deep breath as she saw the determination mirrored on the faces surrounding her. "That's why it's so important that we stay focused and work together. We need to have each other's backs, no matter what."

"Damn right," Hank interjected, his expression fierce. "We got this, Max."

"Definitely," Jules added, her voice soft but resolute.

"Remember, not everything is going to go according to plan. We might encounter unexpected obstacles or challenges along the way," Max warned, her gaze intense. "But I trust each and every one of you to adapt and overcome. We've trained for this. We're ready."

"Max," Sam spoke up, concern etched on his face. "What if they hurt Lexi or Will before we can get to them?"

Her heart clenched at the thought, but she didn't

let her fear show. Instead, she offered Sam a slight smile. "That's why we're going to move fast and smart. We've analyzed the warehouses, we know the potential risks, and we've prepared for them. But I can't stress this enough: stay sharp, stay focused, and stay together."

As they dispersed to double-check their gear, Max allowed herself a brief moment of introspection. She knew that Lexi was more than just a mission objective to her—she had become someone Max cared about deeply. The thought of losing her ignited a fire in Max's chest, fueling her resolve to bring everyone back safely.

"Max," Sam said, breaking into her thoughts. "You alright?"

She looked at him, saw the genuine concern in his eyes, and nodded. "Yeah. Just...let's make sure we bring them home."

"Absolutely," he answered, his voice full of conviction. "We won't let you down."

"Alright, listen up," she commanded, drawing her team's attention back to the task at hand. "We don't have a lot of time until the deadline given for Congresswoman Marsh to withdraw from the campaign. That gives us a tight window to find Lexi and Will, extract them, and neutralize the threat."

Her gaze swept over each member of the assembled group, taking in their expressions of resolve and determination. Sam, Hank, and Jules stood ready, armed with their tactical expertise and staunch loyalty.

She could feel the heaviness of responsibility bearing down on her shoulders, and the thought of Lexi in the hands of the henchmen ignited a spark deep within her. She knew she had to save Lexi, not just for the sake of the mission, but also because she couldn't bear the thought of losing her.

"Let's do this."

As they exited the van, the air crackled with tension, each step taking Max closer to the moment of truth. Max steeled herself, knowing that every decision she made from here on out would shape not only her future, but also the lives of those she cared about most. With a deep breath, she prepared to plunge into the darkness, guided only by her unwavering resolve and the fire burning in her heart.

Chapter Seventeen

The cold air hung thick with tension as Max and her team approached Warehouse C, its looming shadow a promise of danger. With every breath, she could feel the weight of her responsibility bearing down on her. Lexi and Will's lives were in her hands, and she couldn't afford to let them down.

"Stay sharp," Max whispered into her mic, her eyes never leaving the dark entrance before them. "This is it."

"Roger that," Hank replied.

Taking one last deep breath, Max gave the signal. Like a well-oiled machine, the team sprang into action, storming the warehouse with guns drawn and adrenaline pumping.

"Go, go, go!" Max commanded.

As they entered the gloomy depths of the building, a fierce firefight ensued. Bullets whizzed past their heads, the sound of gunfire echoing mercilessly through the cavernous space. Max gritted her teeth, desperately trying to pinpoint the enemy's location amid the chaos.

"Max, I see them!" Jules called out, dodging a hail of bullets as she returned fire. "East side!"

"Got it!" Max shouted back, her mind racing as she formulated a plan. She needed to get to Lexi and Will, but first, they had to neutralize the threat.

"Jules, Hank, keep them pinned down. I'll find

a way there," Max ordered, her eyes searching for a staircase or any means of reaching the second level.

"Be careful, Max," Hank warned, concern lacing his voice as he continued to provide cover fire.

"Always am," she replied, her heart pounding in her chest. As she spotted a rickety set of stairs, she couldn't help but think of Lexi. They'd been through so much together, and the thought of losing her was almost unbearable. Shaking off the fear, Max focused on the task at hand—getting to Lexi and Will alive.

With every step, Max's resolve strengthened. Her mind raced with strategies and possible outcomes while her heart ached for the woman she'd grown to care for deeply. The stakes had never been higher, and as bullets continued to fly and the sound of gunfire filled her ears, Max knew that failure wasn't an option.

"Almost there," she whispered, pushing herself to move faster despite the fatigue creeping into her limbs. "Just hold on, Lexi. I'm coming."

※ ※ ※ ※

Inside the warehouse, Lexi and Will heard the chaos outside, their breaths hitching as they listened to the gunfire. They exchanged wide-eyed glances before instinctively rocking in their chairs, trying to tip them onto the floor so they might have some semblance of shelter from the crossfire. Lexi's heart pounded in her chest, a mix of fear and hope coursing through her veins. Lexi strained against the chains keeping her bound to the chair. She struggled to break free but it was no use.

"Max?" she said, her voice barely audible above the cacophony of gunshots. "Do you think she's out there?"

Will's face paled, but he managed a shaky nod. "She won't let anything happen to us, Lexi. I know it."

"Keep your head down, Will," she instructed, her voice firm despite the tremor she couldn't quite suppress. "We'll get through this."

As the seconds stretched into minutes, Lexi closed her eyes, praying that Max would find them in time.

Finally, the gunfire subsided, replaced by an eerie silence that sent chills down Lexi's spine. Her heart raced faster as she strained to hear any indication of what was happening outside the room they were confined in.

The door to the room burst open, revealing a disheveled and panting Max in its frame. Her eyes locked onto Lexi and Will, still tied to their chairs. Relief mixed with determination washed over her face.

"Max!" Lexi cried out, her eyes filling with tears at the sight of her friend and protector. "Oh, thank God."

"Are you both okay?" Max asked urgently, rushing over to them and assessing their condition with a trained eye.

"Nothing a little duct tape can't fix," Will said weakly. Max huffed a small laugh, but her eyes remained serious as she carefully cut through their bindings.

"Jules and Hank are securing the area. We need to get you both out of here," Max said, her voice tense with urgency. She helped Lexi and Will to their feet, her touch lingering on Lexi's arm just a moment longer than necessary. Lexi's heart fluttered at the contact, even under such dire circumstances.

"Thank you, Max," Lexi whispered, her eyes

searching Max's for a moment before they were interrupted by the sound of footsteps approaching.

"Max, we've got a clear path, but we need to hurry. I have no idea where the others are." Jules announced, poking her head into the room. "Let's get them out of here."

"Right." Max nodded. "Let's move."

༄ ༄ ༄ ༄

The moon cast an eerie glow over the warehouse and cargo container yard, its beams illuminating the scene like nature's own spotlight. Max spotted a stack of crates nearby and bolted toward it. The crates were made of sturdy wood, large enough to hold heavy machinery and supplies, with faded shipping labels barely visible on their sides. They formed a safe fortress among the chaos, providing just enough cover for her to catch her breath and assess the situation.

"Lexi! Will! Stay down!" she shouted, her voice a mix of authority and concern.

From behind the crates, Max peered at the battleground before her. The kidnappers moved with practiced efficiency; their weapons pointed menacingly in every direction. She could see their eyes glinting with cold determination as they scanned the area, searching for any sign of their prey. It was clear that they were well-trained, but Max had been in far worse situations during her time in the army.

"I have two in view," she whispered under her breath, steeling herself for the fight ahead.

As the attackers advanced, Max and her team sprang into action. She launched herself from behind the crates, her weapon raised and ready. Her first shot found its mark, taking down one of the men with a sickening thud. The second attacker turned toward her, only to have his weapon knocked out of his hands by a perfectly aimed bullet from Sam. He barely had time to react before another shot rang out, silencing him permanently.

"Is everyone alright?" Max asked through gritted teeth, ducking back behind the crates for cover.

"Alive," Lexi replied, her voice shaking slightly. "For now."

"Good," Max said, her mind racing with tactical plans. "We need to keep moving. I'll lead, you two follow close behind."

As Max continued to engage the remaining men, she moved like a panther on the prowl. She slid behind the cargo container, her head on a swivel. Even as bullets whizzed past her head, Max remained singularly focused on getting Lexi and Will out safely. With renewed vigor, Max continued to pick off the thugs one by one. Their numbers were dwindling, but so was the ammunition in her weapon. She knew that every shot needed to count if they were going to make it out of this alive.

Her keen senses detected movement to her left—three remaining thugs were attempting to flank her. They moved cautiously, their silhouettes barely visible against the faint moonlight. One carried an automatic rifle, while the other two brandished handguns.

"Stay down," Max warned through gritted teeth, her eyes never leaving the approaching threat. Her mind raced as she calculated their trajectory and weighed her options.

She reached into her vest and pulled out a grenade. She knew there was no room for error—it had to be perfect. As the men drew closer, Max's heart pounded in tandem with their footsteps.

"Everyone, cover your ears," she instructed, her hands trembling ever so slightly as she pulled the pin. With a deep breath, she hurled the grenade toward the unsuspecting assailants.

The projectile arced through the air, its path illuminated by the briefest of sparks. It landed precisely where Max had intended, just between the three enemies. In that split second, their eyes widened with fear, realizing their fatal mistake.

The explosion was deafening, even with their ears covered. A shockwave rippled through the air, sending shattered debris flying in all directions. Flames licked at the edges of the blast radius, illuminating the cloud of smoke that enveloped the scene.

"Is it over?" Will asked hesitantly, his voice trembling.

"Stay here," Max said before she sprinted off to survey the scene.

The aftermath of the explosion left a hazy cloud of smoke hanging in the air, obscuring Max's view of the battlefield. The acrid stench of burnt metal and gunpowder filled her nostrils as she cautiously assessed the situation, her fingers still gripping her weapon tightly.

"Max?" Lexi's voice called out hesitantly from their hiding spot, the concern for her safety evident in her tone.

"Stay down!" Max barked in response, her eyes still scanning the area through the dissipating smoke. She wasn't about to let anything happen to Lexi or Will while there was still a chance that any men remained.

Moments later, the smoke began to clear,

revealing the true extent of the destruction caused by the grenade. Shattered pieces of wood and twisted metal were scattered across the ground, some still smoldering from the blast. The lifeless bodies of the remaining kidnappers lay strewn among the wreckage, their weapons lying dormant beside them.

"Clear," Max finally announced, her voice firm and laced with relief. She raised her free hand, giving a thumbs-up signal toward the direction of Lexi and Will's hiding place.

Peeking out from behind the cargo container, Lexi locked eyes with Max, her eyes shining with gratitude. "Thank you," she mouthed silently before helping Will up from the ground. They emerged from their cover, both visibly shaken but unharmed.

"Are you two okay?" Max asked, her heart pounding in her chest as she took in their disheveled appearances.

꙳꙳꙳꙳

Lexi brushed the dust and debris from her clothes, while Will gingerly held his arm. They exchanged nervous glances, relief and fear mingling in their eyes.

"Is it over?" Will asked, his voice barely above a whisper.

"Seems like it," Lexi replied, her gaze fixed on Max as she approached them, her weapon still at the ready. "For now."

Max studied their faces, looking for any signs of pain or injury. "You two alright?"

"Other than feeling like I just aged ten years in five minutes, yeah," Lexi quipped, attempting to lighten the mood. Her expression grew serious as she noticed Will's arm and the wound that looked like a bullet graze. "Will, you're hurt."

"It's just a scratch," he said, dismissing it with a shrug, but the wince that followed betrayed the pain he was in.

"Let me take a look," Max insisted, her concern evident.

"Thanks again, Max," Will said, his bravado momentarily dampened by gratitude. "I owe you one."

"Let's just make sure this doesn't happen again," Max replied firmly, her eyes meeting Lexi's.

"Agreed," Lexi said, determination simmering beneath the surface. "We've got a long road ahead of us, though. We don't even know if we got them all."

"I'll get everyone involved. Don't worry. They made it personal," Max stated, her words reflecting her resolve.

As the three of them stood there, battered but unbroken, Lexi knew that the fight was far from over. There were still questions to be answered, enemies to face, and a campaign—not to mention their own lives—hanging in the balance.

⚜⚜⚜⚜

Max dialed the number and waited for the voice on the other side.

"Max, please tell me you have them."

"Congresswoman Marsh," Max said, her voice steady and reassuring. "I've found Lexi and Will. They're safe."

"Thank God," Marsh whispered, her voice thick with emotion. "Thank you, Max. Thank you so much."

"You're welcome, Congresswoman."

Chapter Eighteen

Shadows flickered on the wall of the safehouse's bedroom as the small candle on the table danced in the draft. Max paced, her breaths coming in short, measured bursts. Lexi, pale and trembling, sat on the edge of the bed, her arms wrapped around herself for comfort. The air between them crackled with an unspoken tension.

"Are you sure you're okay?" Max asked, her voice barely a whisper. She stopped pacing and stood in front of Lexi, her eyes filled with concern.

Lexi looked up, her eyes meeting Max's gaze. "I can't believe what's just happened, Max."

"I know, but you're safe now," Max said.

"How did it go?"

"Well, they were able to deliver the bodies of the assholes who kidnapped you to the safe keeping of the police," Max smiled down at Lexi.

"Who were they?"

"Best I can guess, after running their faces and prints through our system…a paramilitary group from the drug cartels."

"What about Brown and Guevara?"

"They've gone underground."

"Christ, so we're not out of danger yet?"

"I'm sorry, Lexi. We're doing our best to find them. Don't worry, we'll get them. How are you feeling?"

"I'm just shaken up," she admitted, her voice quivering. "But I'll be fine. What time is it?"

"Late. Here." Max grabbed a blanket from the foot of the bed and draped it over Lexi's shoulders. Their fingers brushed briefly, and Lexi's heart fluttered at the contact.

"Thanks," Lexi murmured, pulling the blanket tighter around her. She couldn't help but notice how Max's eyes lingered on her face, tracing every curve and angle.

The heavy silence in the room was broken only by their soft breaths, and the dim light filtering through the curtains cast eerie shadows on the walls, amplifying their sense of vulnerability.

Lexi's hands trembled as she clenched them into fists, her knuckles white. She fought to keep her emotions at bay, knowing she needed to be strong. Yet, deep inside, a whirlwind of fear and anger threatened to consume her.

"Hey," Max said softly.

"Yes," Lexi replied, her voice barely above a whisper.

Max nodded, her gaze locked to Lexi's. "I'm here for you, Lexi. Whatever you need, okay? Just say the word."

"Thank you," Lexi whispered, her eyes filling with tears as she registered Max's sincerity. "I don't know what I would do without you."

"Let's not find out," Max replied, a rare half smile tugging at the corners of her mouth. She gently took Lexi's hand in her own, giving it a firm squeeze. "I meant what I said. I'll do whatever it takes to help you and Will through this."

As Max spoke, Lexi felt a small flicker of hope ignite within her chest. The warmth of Max's touch seemed to chase away some of the shadows that had enveloped her heart, allowing her to glimpse a future where healing was possible.

"Thank you, again," Lexi repeated, her eyes glistening with gratitude as she looked up at Max. In that moment, she knew they were connected by something deeper than friendship—a bond that would carry them through this storm and beyond.

"Always," Max whispered, her voice barely audible as she leaned in to press a gentle kiss to Lexi's forehead. The soft contact sent a shiver down Lexi's spine, but it was a welcome sensation—a reminder that she was alive and that love could still bloom amid the darkness.

❧ ❧ ❧ ❧ ❧

Max watched Lexi closely, her eyes full of concern as she took in the tense lines of Lexi's face, the way her fingers clenched and unclenched around the edge of the blanket draped over her shoulders.

"Lexi," Max said gently, breaking the quiet that had settled between them. "I know things are tough right now, but I think it might be a good idea for you and Will to consider seeking professional help, maybe some counseling. It's important to address your trauma, so you can heal and move forward."

For a moment, Lexi just stared at her, the vulnerability in her eyes so raw it threatened to break Max's heart. Then, slowly, she nodded, her voice barely more than a whisper as she replied, "You're right, Max. I...I need help."

"Hey." Max reached out and touched Lexi's arm, her grip firm yet gentle. "There's no shame in admitting that. What you and Will went through would leave anyone struggling. But you don't have to face it alone."

A tear slid down Lexi's cheek, and this time, she didn't bother trying to hide it or brush it away. Instead, she looked directly at Max, her gaze steady and full of gratitude. "Thank you, Max. For everything. You've been my rock through all of this, and I...I don't know how to say how much that means to me."

"Lexi, you don't need to say anything, and you can stop thanking me," Max replied softly, her own eyes glistening with unshed tears. "Just knowing I could be there for you, that I could help you even in the smallest way—it means the world to me too."

Something shifted between them, a subtle change in the air that hinted at the potential for something more. It was a moment of connection, one that spoke not only to the struggle but also of a bond that had deepened through adversity.

"Promise me..." Lexi whispered, her voice trembling as she reached out to grasp Max's hand, her fingers warm and slightly shaking. "Promise me you'll be there, no matter what comes next."

"I promise, Lexi," Max replied without hesitation, her grip tightening around Lexi's hand. "No matter what, we'll face it together. And we'll come through it stronger than ever."

At that moment, when their eyes locked, Max felt a silent understanding pass between them. Not just a pledge of support and friendship, but something deeper. Even though she was aware that the journey ahead would come with its share of difficulties—traumatic events always did—Max was determined, resolute, and ready to tackle whatever came their way.

⚜⚜⚜⚜

The room seemed to shrink around Lexi as she tried to summon the courage to ask for what she really wanted. She wasn't sure if she could have all of Max, but she would settle for everything Max was willing to give. Lexi longed for the feel of Max's arms around her again…for however long it lasted.

"Please stay with me? Just…just as friends," Lexi added hastily, her cheeks flushing with embarrassment as she'd tried to thread the needle between desperate and nonchalant and was mortified to discover she'd failed miserably.

"Of course," Max replied softly, the corners of her mouth lifting in a gentle smile that reached her eyes. "I'll be right here."

As Max settled down beside Lexi on the bed, they leaned into each other, their shoulders touching, the warmth of their bodies providing solace in a world gone cold. They stayed that way for a time, wrapped in silence and the fragile comfort of each other's presence.

"Listen, Lexi," Max started, hesitating for a moment before continuing. "I…I need to say this. I care about you. A lot."

"Max," Lexi whispered, her cheeks flushing with warmth. "I—"

"More than I should," Max confessed, moving closer. "And it scares me."

"Me too," Lexi admitted, her pulse quickening as Max closed the distance between them. "But maybe that's not such a bad thing."

"Maybe," Max conceded, her voice husky with desire. "But right now, we have to stay focused."

As the night wore on, the silence in the room grew heavier, each passing moment a reminder of the danger lurking beyond their sanctuary. Max's hand grazed Lexi's knee, sending shivers up her spine. Lexi inhaled sharply, swallowing the moan that threatened to escape her lips.

"Lexi," Max breathed, her words like a plea for understanding. "I want you so badly it hurts."

"Max," Lexi murmured, her heart racing as she looked into those intense eyes. "I want you too."

"Then let's not fight it anymore." Max's voice was filled with longing.

"Let's not."

But just as their lips were about to meet, a distant crash echoed through the safe house, shattering the fragile peace they'd found in each other's arms. Lexi pulled away abruptly, her emotions quickly shifting from desire to self-preservation.

"Stay here," Max ordered as she grabbed her weapon, her eyes scanning the room for any potential threats.

"Be careful," Lexi whispered as she watched Max leave, her heart lodged painfully in her throat.

As Lexi sat there, her body still humming with unfulfilled desire, she knew that even in the face of danger, her connection with Max could not be denied. And neither could the promise of what might come once the storm had passed.

Max came back into the room with a smile on her face.

"What happened?"

"Will was trying to make coffee and he dropped a cup."

"Oh, geez. I should help him."

"He's fine. Relax. Now where were we?" Max held Lexi.

Slowly, they leaned in, their lips brushing softly,

tentatively. It was a fleeting kiss, barely a touch, but it spoke volumes for Lexi. They drew back, eyes wide with surprise and something more—something that she didn't want to think about at this moment.

"Let's get some rest," Max suggested, smoothing a stray lock of hair away from Lexi's face. "Tomorrow is a new day, and we'll need our strength."

As they curled up together on the bed, Lexi nestled against Max's shoulder, sleep beckoning like a gentle embrace. For the first time in weeks, she allowed herself to believe that maybe, just maybe, they could emerge from this darkness, scarred but unbroken. And as she drifted off to the sound of Max's steady heartbeat, Lexi knew deep down that whatever trials lay ahead, they would face them hand in hand, hearts united in purpose and resolve.

ৠৠৠৠ

The sun was just peeking in the sky when Max awoke, her body instinctively on high alert. She disentangled herself from Lexi's embrace, careful not to disturb her as she slept. The soft, orange glow of the early light bathed the room in a warm hue, casting long shadows across the floor.

Today, Max thought, steeling herself for the challenges that lay ahead. *We put an end to this.*

Her gaze fell upon Lexi's peaceful face, a stark contrast to the turmoil they'd faced together. The vulnerability in her expression tugged at Max's heart, but it also fueled her determination to protect her at all costs.

"Max?" Lexi mumbled, stirring from sleep. She blinked up at Max, her eyes hazy with drowsiness.

"What time is it?"

"Early," Max replied softly, brushing Lexi's hair back from her forehead. "I need to meet with Congresswoman Marsh and get the ball rolling on our next move. A team is here at the safehouse and will keep you secure while I'm gone."

"Okay." Lexi sighed, rubbing the sleep from her eyes. "Just be careful, please."

"Always," Max promised, pressing a gentle kiss to Lexi's temple before slipping out of the room.

As Max made her way down the hallway of the campaign offices, she caught snippets of hushed conversations between Sarah, Ethan, and other members of Congresswoman Marsh's team, their voices tense with anticipation. It was clear that the pressure was mounting, and the stakes were higher than ever.

"Max," Congresswoman Marsh called out once she spotted her, beckoning her over. "Any news on Dan Brown and this drug cartel kingpin?"

"Not yet," Max said, frustration simmering beneath the surface. "But we're closing in. We'll find them, Congresswoman. I promise."

Marsh scrutinized Max for a moment, her eyes filled with a mix of gratitude and concern. "Thank you, Max. You've already done so much to keep Lexi and Will safe."

"Nothing's going to happen to them on my watch," Max vowed, her voice steady with conviction. "But we need to act fast. Time's running out."

"Agreed." Congresswoman Marsh nodded, her expression resolute. "Let's gather everyone and start planning our response."

As they moved from room to room assembling the team, Max couldn't shake the nagging feeling that the enemy was closer than they realized. She knew they had to stay vigilant, anticipating every possible scenario.

"Congresswoman Marsh," Ethan interjected, his brow furrowed as he read a message on his phone. "I just got word that Jenny's gone missing. Her family hasn't heard from her for two days."

"Damn it," the congresswoman muttered under her breath, clearly thrown by the news. "We need Jenny found. That bitch needs to pay for what she's done to my son and Lexi. Find her."

"I agree and we're doing our best to find her, Congresswoman," Max countered, her mind racing with possibilities. "Jenny's disappearance might be the least of our immediate worries, but we know she was involved in the plot and we will stake out her apartment, her job, her family's house—anywhere she might have gone underground. Don't worry, she's at the top of my list. I can assure you of that."

"Max is right," Sarah chimed in, her gaze locked on Congresswoman Marsh. "We have to consider every angle."

"Fine," Congresswoman Marsh conceded, her jaw clenched with determination. "Let's get to work."

As the team dove into strategizing their next steps, Max couldn't help but let her thoughts drift back to Lexi, wondering if she'd ever truly be safe from the shadows that threatened to consume them. But she clung to the promise they'd made to each other, the unspoken connection that bound them together in the face of adversity.

Chapter Nineteen

The soft hum of the air-conditioning was the only sound that filled the hallway as Max made her way toward the sounds of a gurgling coffee machine. As she poured herself a cup, she heard Lexi enter the safehouse's kitchen behind her. She turned, her heart wrenching when she saw the dried trail of tears that marked Lexi's face.

"Hey, you okay?" Max said, stepping closer.

"Rough night."

"It's to be expected. You've been through a lot."

Their fingers brushed against each other, sending an electric thrill up Max's arm and making her heart race. The connection between them felt undeniable, a magnetic force drawing them closer with each step.

Without saying a word, Lexi pulled Max toward her bedroom.

Max noticed the shift in Lexi's disposition and offered a reassuring smile. As Max reached for the doorknob, Lexi hesitated before reaching out to stop her, placing her hand over Max's for a brief moment. The warmth of Lexi's touch sparked another jolt of electricity between them, the sensation lingering even after Lexi pulled away.

"Max," Lexi began, her voice filled with vulnerability and longing. "Would you stay with me? Just for a little while?"

Max searched Lexi's eyes for any hint of uncertainty but instead found a desperate need for closeness and comfort. Their situation hung heavy on both of their shoulders, the stakes higher than ever with the threat of blackmail looming over Congresswoman Marsh's campaign. She knew Will's previous drug dealing could come back and hand Marsh a defeat, but that was the least of their worries.

"Of course," Max replied softly, her voice steady and resolute despite the pounding of her heart. "I'll stay with you."

As they entered the dimly lit room, the world outside seemed to fade away, leaving behind only the two of them and the intimate space. The smell of lavender and vanilla floated through the air, calming Max's racing thoughts as she tried to focus on the task at hand—protecting Lexi—but her mind wandered to how she had quickly come to need this beautiful woman and wanted to always be around her.

"Thank you," Lexi whispered, her eyes shining with unshed tears as she squeezed Max's hand, intertwining their fingers in a silent declaration of their connection.

"Of course." Max's   heart pounded with anticipation as she lay down on the bed next to Lexi.

"Max, I can't tell you how much it means for you to be here with me right now," Lexi said quietly, her voice thick with emotion.

"Hey, it's my job to protect you," Max replied, attempting a lighthearted tone despite the depth of her feelings. "And besides, I want to be here with you, too."

"Is it really just part of your job?" Lexi asked with a small smile, challenging Max's words gently.

"Maybe not entirely," Max admitted. Her eyes locked with Lexi's, sharing in the vulnerability of the moment. She felt a sudden urge to reach out and touch

Lexi's hand but hesitated, unsure if such a gesture would be welcome or appropriate given their current circumstances.

"Max," Lexi began again, a glimmer of hope shining through her uncertain expression. "I want to believe that there's more to us than just this…this danger we faced. I've thought about you every time I see you, and I can't help but wonder what might happen between us if things were different."

"Lexi," Max whispered, her chest tightening at the sincerity in Lexi's voice. The desire to protect Lexi and keep her safe was intertwined with something deeper, something Max couldn't quite put into words yet. She struggled to find the right response, her thoughts racing with the implications of their actions.

"Maybe it's too soon to talk about this," Lexi continued, her eyes searching Max's face for clues to her inner turmoil. "But I just needed to say it, to let you know how much I care about you, and how much I want to explore whatever connection we have."

"Lexi, I…I feel the same way," Max confessed, her voice barely audible as she finally reached out and took Lexi's hand in hers. The warmth of their intertwined fingers sent a jolt of electricity through Max's body, igniting a fire within her that threatened to consume her entirely.

"Then let's not waste any more time," Lexi said softly.

As they lay there, side by side, Max couldn't help but think about what the future might hold for them. Their growing love was like a quiet storm, building slowly beneath the surface, waiting for the right moment to unleash its full force. And in the quiet, dark room, with Lexi's hand in hers, Max had never felt more alive.

ꗨꗨꗨꗨ

The air around them seemed to hum with anticipation as Lexi's hand, still holding Max's, moved softly across her skin. Tracing delicate patterns along the curve of Max's ribs, each touch was like a whispered secret, stirring an unspoken language between them.

"Lexi," Max breathed, her voice barely audible. The fire within Lexi roared to life, ignited by the tender exploration of her fingertips.

"Max," Lexi murmured, her eyes communicating a question she couldn't quite put into words. "Can I keep going?"

"Please," Max said.

Lexi felt both vulnerable and empowered by the trust they were placing in one another. Her heart pounded in her chest, the rhythm almost deafening in the intimate space.

As Lexi continued her tender journey, navigating the landscape of Max's body, the room seemed to shrink around them, the walls closing in as if to contain the intensity of their connection. Their breaths mingled, creating a cadence that filled the air, punctuated by brief bursts of action as their limbs tangled together in a dance of discovery.

"Max, are you okay?" Lexi asked, pausing for a moment to gauge her reaction. Her eyes held a mixture of concern and longing that spoke volumes.

"More than okay," Max managed.

"Good," Lexi whispered, her thumb gently stroking Max's wrist as they resumed their exploration. "I don't want to push this, but I just need to feel...I don't know, closer, protected, something."

"Trust me," Max whispered, her breath catching as Lexi resumed her gentle ministrations. "I'll protect you, I promise."

And so, they continued their journey together, their bodies entwining as they forged a connection that transcended words. The outside world faded away, leaving only the raw power of their emotions and the rhythm of their hearts, beating in perfect harmony.

The dimly lit room seemed to glow with an ethereal light as they moved closer together, their bodies speaking a language all their own. Passion and tenderness intermingled, creating a symphony of sensation that filled every inch of her body.

"Lexi, I need you," Max breathed, her voice trembling with her confession.

"Max, I need you, too," Lexi replied, tears glistening in her eyes as she echoed the sentiment.

⚘⚘⚘⚘

As smoldering desire coursed through her veins, Max's breath hitched at Lexi's tender touch.

"Come here," Max whispered, pulling Lexi closer until their bodies aligned in a dance of longing and anticipation, an unspoken promise that even amid the chaos of the political world outside, they had a connection worth exploring more deeply.

"Max, I can feel your heartbeat racing," Lexi murmured, her voice filled with vulnerability as she laid her hand on Max's chest.

"Yours too," Max replied softly, shifting her hand to rest atop Lexi's. "It's been a long time since I've felt this way."

"Me too," Lexi admitted, a tentative smile playing on her lips. Their vulnerability hung like a delicate thread between them, daring them to unravel it together.

"Can I...?" Lexi began, hesitating only for a moment before gently brushing her fingertips against Max's collarbone, seeking permission.

"Please," Max managed to utter, her pulse quickening. She silently marveled at Lexi's ability to break down the walls she had built over the years, leaving her exposed but not vulnerable.

Slowly and delicately, they explored each other's bodies, guided by something deeper, something Max hadn't felt in a long time. Max's fingers traced the curve of Lexi's jaw, committing every detail to memory. She reveled in the warmth of Lexi's skin beneath her touch and the shiver that ran through Lexi's body as her fingers brushed against the sensitive hollow of her throat.

"Your touch is electrifying," Lexi whispered.

In response, Max leaned in, capturing Lexi's lips with her own, the kiss a testament to their growing bond. As their mouths moved in harmony, Lexi's hands danced along Max's back, fingers pressing into the soft flesh and muscles beneath.

"Max," Lexi said against her lips. "I want to remember everything about this moment, every sensation, every emotion."

"Let's make it unforgettable, then," Max replied, her voice filled with certainty. And as they continued to unravel each other layer by layer, the world outside seemed to fade away, leaving them suspended in a moment where love and desire intertwined, forging a bond that transcended time and space.

They explored each other's bodies for what seemed like an eternity, discovering new sensations and unearthing forgotten passions. Max felt Lexi's spine arch beneath her touch as she explored every contour, searching for the spot that brought Lexi the greatest pleasure. As their dance intensified, so did Max's craving for the taste of each kiss, reveling in the sweet saltiness of desire.

The electricity between them grew stronger with each passing moment, and soon enough Max was urging Lexi closer, unable to quench her thirst for more. She reached a trembling hand up to cup Lexi's face as they kissed passionately, exploring uncharted territories with each passing second. The intensity of it all left Max feeling dizzy, and before long their skin tangled together in an embrace that was both wild and tender at once.

Amid the heat radiating from their bodies came explosions of pleasure so intense that Max could hardly contain it—wave after wave washing over them until she was beyond reason. As they tumbled over the edge into blissful oblivion, whispering words of love into one another's ears, there could be no denial. Something truly special was going on here.

When finally reality slowly seeped back in and Max opened her eyes to gaze into Lexi's again, she felt reborn, cleansed not only by exertion and sweat, but also by emotion.

※.※.※.※.

Lexi awoke to the soft light of the moon filtering through the curtains. She blinked, her mind still heavy with sleep, as she turned her head to find Max beside her. Their night had been a tender exploration of one another, and now Lexi couldn't help but smile at the sight of her slumbering lover.

"Max," Lexi whispered, gently brushing a strand of hair from the other woman's forehead. Max stirred, her eyes fluttering open as she registered Lexi's presence.

"Hey," she mumbled with a sleepy grin.

"Hey," Lexi echoed, her heart swelling with affection. As she gazed into Max's eyes, she found herself once again struck by the depth of their connection. It was as if they had discovered a hidden treasure within each other, and now that they had unlocked its secrets, there was no turning back.

"Last night was…incredible," Max murmured, reaching out to trace the curve of Lexi's cheek.

"I don't know what to say," Lexi replied, feeling a surge of warmth at the sincerity in Max's voice. "I've never felt so close to someone before."

"Neither have I," Max admitted, her gaze locked on Lexi's. "But we need to talk about what this means for us going forward."

"Of course," Lexi said, steeling herself for the conversation she knew they had to have.

"Given our involvement with the congresswoman's campaign and the threats against her, things could get complicated," Max said seriously, her brow furrowed with concern. "We need to tread carefully."

"Absolutely," Lexi agreed, her own worry beginning to rise. "We can't let our personal relationship interfere with our professionalism."

"Right." Max nodded.

"What about Brown and Guevara? What if it all comes out?" Lexi searched Max's face.

"Then we'll face it together," Max replied firmly,

her eyes shining with conviction. "No matter what happens, I'm not going to let anything tear us apart."

"Promise?" Lexi asked, searching Max's face for reassurance.

"Promise," Max vowed, her gaze never wavering. "We're stronger together, remember?"

"Always," Lexi whispered, her heart swelling with love and gratitude. As they lay there, wrapped in each other's arms, she felt secure in the knowledge that they both were determined to face whatever challenges life had in store for them together.

Even so, as the sun continued to rise, casting the room in a golden glow, Lexi couldn't shake the feeling that they were standing on the edge of a precipice, their fates hanging in the balance. And as the morning wore on, her sense of trepidation only grew, leaving her wondering just how far Max was willing to go for love, considering all the walls she'd built to survive as both a soldier and a cop, and to keep herself safe.

Chapter Twenty

The muted hum of conversation and laughter filled the air as Lexi and Max stood among the celebrating crowd. The campaign headquarters was awash in vibrant shades of blue and gold, reflecting Congresswoman Marsh's victory.

"Alright, we should probably talk to the FBI sooner rather than later," Lexi said, her voice steady but tinged with apprehension. "Let's get this over with."

"Agreed," Max replied, offering a reassuring smile. "No matter what they ask, we'll be honest and stick to the truth. We've got nothing to hide, right?"

Lexi nodded, taking a deep breath before turning her gaze to the lively celebration around them.

As the two made their way through the bustling room, they couldn't help but feel overwhelmed by the sheer magnitude of the event. The faces of friends, colleagues, and strangers all blurred together, each one displaying a mixture of joy and relief at the hard-won victory. It was a moment that Lexi had never thought she would experience, and now that it was here, she found herself grappling with a mix of emotions.

"Lexi," Max whispered, leaning closer to her ear. "Remember, we came out on top. Everything that happened led us here."

"Thank you, Max," Lexi murmured, feeling her heart swell with gratitude for the woman who had become her rock in recent weeks.

As they reached the door where two solemn-looking FBI agents awaited them, Lexi gave Max's hand a quick squeeze before stepping forward.

"Agents," she greeted, her voice firm and confident. "We're ready to cooperate and provide you with all the details of the blackmail plot."

"Thank you," said one agent, nodding appreciatively. "Please, follow us."

The interview that followed was intense and exhausting, but Lexi and Max remained steadfast in their determination to bring the truth to light. They recounted every detail, every threat, and every harrowing moment that had led them to this point.

"Thank you for your cooperation," the agents said as they wrapped up their questions. "You've provided us with valuable information. We'll be in touch if we need anything further."

"Of course," Lexi replied, trying to hide the fatigue in her voice. "We're just glad to help put an end to this nightmare."

"Me too," Max added, giving Lexi a warm, supportive smile.

As they left the interrogation room and reentered the celebration, it felt as though a weight had been lifted from their shoulders. They were no longer bound by the secrets and lies that had once threatened to tear them apart.

"Come on," Max said gently, guiding Lexi back into the throng of partygoers. "Let's enjoy this victory."

Together, they lost themselves in the sea of jubilant faces, taking solace in one another's presence as they let the music and laughter wash over them. The night was filled with heartfelt congratulations, smiles, and few quiet moments of reflection, all underscored by an undeniable sense of relief.

"Max," Lexi whispered at one point, leaning close so she could be heard above the din. "I just want you to know...I'm grateful for everything you've done for me. For us."

"Same here, Lexi," Max replied, her eyes shining with sincerity. "We got through this together, and now we can face whatever comes next."

Their gazes locked, and for a fleeting moment, the world around them seemed to fade away. It was just Lexi and Max, standing strong against the tide, their hearts intertwined in a bond forged by love, loyalty, and triumph.

"Want to get out of here?" Lexi suggested, her eyes searching Max's face.

"Definitely," Max agreed, relief flooding her features.

❦❦❦❦

The streetlights cast a warm glow on the pavement outside Lexi's home, their flickering shadows dancing in tandem with the rustling leaves of the trees that lined the quiet suburban street. As Lexi unlocked her front door, Max couldn't help but notice the way the golden light caught in the strands of Lexi's brown hair, giving her an almost ethereal appearance. The moment was suspended like a droplet of amber, and Max found herself holding her breath, captivated by the woman beside her.

"Here we are," Lexi murmured, pushing open the door to reveal the cozy interior of her home. "Please, make yourself comfortable."

"Thank you," Max replied softly.

As Lexi closed the door behind them, Max

couldn't help but feel a small shiver of anticipation race down her spine. Being alone with Lexi in her home felt both thrilling and nerve-wracking, a potent mixture of emotions that left her feeling slightly dizzy. She took a deep breath, trying to steady herself as she turned to face Lexi.

"Would you like something to drink?" Lexi offered, her voice wavering only slightly as she visibly tried to maintain a semblance of composure.

"Actually, I'd prefer if we could just…talk," Max replied, her eyes full of sincerity. "I want to know more about you, and what brought you here."

"Didn't we already have this conversation?" Lexi said as she led Max to the couch, where they sat down, side by side. Their knees brushed against one another, sending a jolt of electricity through Max.

"Well…." Max's eyes twinkled.

"Okay," Lexi began, her voice soft and reflective. "Before all this I was just a college graduate with big dreams and a passion for politics. I never imagined I'd be part of something so much bigger than myself."

"Neither did I," Max admitted, the quiet intensity of her gaze holding Lexi captive. She reached out, gently taking Lexi's hand in hers.

"Me either," Lexi whispered, her eyes shining with unshed tears. She leaned in, and Max met her halfway, their lips brushing together in a tender, almost reverent kiss.

In that moment, all the noise and commotion of the world seemed to fall away, leaving only the two of them entwined in each other's arms. The kiss deepened, becoming a passionate exchange of unspoken promises and desires.

Later, as they lay tangled together in Lexi's

bed, the moonlight casting a silver glow over their intertwined forms, Max traced delicate patterns on Lexi's arm. "What do you think the future holds for us?" she asked, her voice barely above a whisper.

"I don't know for sure," Lexi admitted   . "But I do know that whatever comes I want to be by your side."

"Promise?" Max asked, her heart swelling with love and devotion for the woman beside her. She searched Lexi's face for reassurance.

"Promise," Lexi replied, sealing her vow with another gentle kiss.

A warmth blossomed like a delicate flower between them, nurtured by the strength of their connection and devotion. As they lay there, wrapped in each other's embrace, Max hoped that Lexi would in fact be part of her future.

The moonlit room was a sanctuary, the muted glow casting long shadows that seemed to hold their secrets. Lexi and Max lay entwined on the bed, their bodies gradually cooling as they whispered of dreams, fears, and hopes.

"My love," Lexi murmured, her voice trembling with emotion. "I've never felt so connected to anyone before."

"Me neither," Max admitted, a vulnerability she rarely allowed herself to reveal shining through her words. "But it's not enough, is it? Just talking about our feelings isn't going to make the world outside go away."

"Sometimes," Lexi said softly, tracing the curve of Max's cheek with her fingertips. "You need to let actions speak louder than words."

In response, Max leaned in, capturing Lexi's lips with her own. The kiss was slow and deep, allowing them to taste each other's souls, to revel in the love that had grown between them. Their hands roamed, gently exploring the landscapes of one another's bodies, rekindling the fire that had burned brightly just moments before.

As their passion reignited, Lexi whispered into Max's ear, "Let me show you how much you mean to me." The words were an invitation, a tender request for permission, and Max nodded, her eyes locked onto Lexi's.

Their lovemaking was different this time, less frantic and more deliberate. Each touch, each caress, carried the urgency of something shared, anchoring them to one another. With every gasp and sigh, Max could feel their connection, the power of their lovemaking wrapping around them like a protective shield.

Afterward, Max struggled to find words to give voice to her emotions. She settled on the only truth she knew for certain. "I can't imagine my life without you."

"Neither can I," Lexi replied, her own voice tight with emotion.

As their breathing slowed and their heartbeats began to return to normal, Lexi and Max lay entwined on the bed, their eyes locked in a gaze that spoke volumes.

"Whatever challenges lie ahead," Lexi whispered, her hand finding Max's and giving it a gentle squeeze. "I know we have each other. And that's all that matters."

"Always," Max agreed.

And as the moon continued its nightly journey across the sky, casting ever-changing shadows upon them, Max knew that no matter what the future held, Lexi would be by her side.

Chapter Twenty-one

I know you've had a lot on your plate these past few months, Lexi. How's your   mom doing?"

"Good, Congresswoman. She's on the road to recovery, thank God."

"That's great news."

"How is Will doing?" Lexi realized she hadn't asked about him in a while. In fact, as bad as it sounded, she hadn't thought about him either. She guessed it was a part of her life she was compartmentalizing until she could get some counseling and unpack those bags with a professional. Now, she felt bad she hadn't been better about staying connected. She knew he must have been going through something similar, and she couldn't imagine dealing with the betrayal of a girlfriend on top of everything else.

"He's...he's doing okay. I'm not sure he's even close to dealing with what Jenny did. I'm not sure any of us are, really, but he seems to be doing okay."

"That's good. Can you tell him I'm always here if he needs a shoulder? I mean, we went through this together, and I would hate to think he wouldn't reach out...well, you know what I mean."

"I think I do. So, I need to talk to you, but most importantly, I'd really like you to come to the swearing-in celebration tomorrow night. If, of course, you're feeling up to it."

"Sure. It'll be great to see everyone."

"That's my girl. I'll see you tomorrow?"

"Okay," Lexi said, closing her phone.

"Who was that, honey?" Cynthia said, smiling at her. Her mother had been sleeping through her final chemo treatment.

"Congresswoman Marsh. She wants me to stop by the office tomorrow."

"Go. You don't need to babysit me. Besides, your father has taken the day off. Something about treating me to a spa day or something."

"Seriously?"

Cynthia had finally come clean with her husband. He'd shocked them all when he announced he would be taking a leave of absence from work.

"Yep."

"Wow, he has really surprised me."

"You? He surprised me, too." Cynthia watched as the nurse took the IV out of her chest.

"You won't need this anymore." The nurse smiled. "We're going to miss you, Cynthia."

"Yeah, but if I'm honest. I won't miss this," she said, tapping the port in her chest.

"It'll come out soon."

"Not soon enough for me."

"That's what they all say." The nurse smiled over at Lexi. "She'll be a little weak for the rest of the week, so make sure she rests."

"Oh, I will." Lexi folded the blanket and put it on the chair her mom had just vacated. "I will."

Lexi tucked her mom's arm through hers. "Let's go get a coffee."

"Will Max be there?"

"Maybe, if I call her to meet us."

"Call her. I like Max." Cynthia patted Lexi's arm. "She's good for you."

"Uh-huh."

❧❧❧❧

The grand ballroom of the historic Hotel Royale shimmered with golden light as Lexi and Max arrived at the celebratory dinner for Congresswoman Marsh's swearing in. Crystal chandeliers cast a warm glow over the elegantly dressed guests, reflecting off the polished marble floors like stars in a night sky. The atmosphere was electric, anticipation and excitement filled the air, mingling with the soft hum of conversation and the clinking of champagne glasses.

"Wow," breathed Lexi, her eyes wide with wonder. "This place is incredible."

Max squeezed Lexi's hand gently, her eyes vibrant with admiration. "Congresswoman Marsh certainly knows how to throw a party," she said, guiding Lexi through the throng of guests.

Hand in hand, Lexi and Max navigated the sea of tailored suits and opulent gowns, their love for each other evident in the way they moved together, perfectly in sync. Lexi leaned in close to Max, her voice barely audible over the din of the crowd. "I don't think I've ever been so happy," she admitted, her cheeks flushing with warmth.

"Me neither," Max whispered back, her grip on Lexi's hand tightening just a fraction, conveying more than words could express.

As they made their way through the room, Lexi felt a swell of pride at being here with Max, the woman she loved. Their journey together had been filled with challenges, but through it all, they had remained steadfast in their devotion to one another.

"Look at us," Lexi murmured, her gaze drifting over the well-heeled attendees. "Who would have thought two scrappy kids like us would end up here?"

"Hey, we earned our place here," Max insisted, her eyes narrowing playfully. "And you know what? We deserve it."

Lexi smiled, her heart swelling with affection. "Damn right we do," she said, giving Max's hand a reassuring squeeze.

Max chuckled softly. "It's a special night, after all. A well-deserved celebration for all the hard work you and Congresswoman Marsh put into the campaign."

"Speaking of which, we should probably go say hello to her before we get too caught up in everything else," Lexi suggested, and Max nodded in agreement.

As they moved farther into the room, Lexi couldn't help but think about the challenges they had faced together. Despite the odds stacked against them, Lexi and Max had emerged victorious, forging an unbreakable bond in the process.

"Lexi! Max!" Congresswoman Marsh called out, her smile genuine as she approached them. "You both look absolutely stunning tonight."

"Thank you, Congresswoman," Lexi replied graciously. "The ballroom looks incredible. Your team has outdone themselves."

"Indeed," Max chimed in. "It's a night to remember."

"Ah, but the night is still young," Marsh said with a knowing smile. "Now, if you'll excuse me, I see some other guests that require my attention. Enjoy your evening!"

As Marsh walked away, Lexi and Max exchanged a confused glance. Lexi wondered why the congresswoman was so...aloof.

The joy and excitement in the grand ballroom was palpable, a tangible energy that seemed to infuse everyone with an electric happiness. Lexi and Max walked hand in hand, their own faces alight with love and contentment, their fingers entwined as if to say they were truly inseparable. Their smiles were infectious, drawing others into their orbit of warmth and affection.

"Max, isn't this incredible?" Lexi whispered, her eyes wide with the wonder of it all. "We're really here, celebrating together."

As they continued through the room, Lexi and Max found themselves greeted by a multitude of well-wishers. The conversations flowed effortlessly, a seamless dance of congratulations and praise punctuated by bouts of laughter.

"Lexi! Max!" a man called out, grinning from ear to ear. "It's great, isn't it?"

"Thank you, but we couldn't have done it without your support when the congresswoman was running her campaign," Lexi replied warmly, squeezing Max's hand reassuringly.

"Absolutely," Max added. "I'm just glad we could be a part of something so important."

"Here, here!" another guest chimed in, raising a glass in salute. There was a murmur of agreement from those nearby, and Lexi felt her cheeks flush pink with pride.

Throughout the evening, Lexi and Max wove their way through the crowd, engaging with friends and acquaintances while always ensuring that they remained close to one another. It was clear to anyone watching that their bond had only grown stronger since the harrowing events that brought them together.

In quieter moments, when the noise and activity around them seemed to fade away, Lexi allowed herself to reflect on the journey she and Max had taken. From their first meeting, through the dangerous encounters with blackmailers and criminals, to the final victory that had secured Congresswoman Marsh's place in office—every step they took had drawn them closer, forging a connection that felt unbreakable.

"Max," Lexi said softly, looking into her partner's eyes, "I can't imagine going through all of this with anyone else. I love you."

Max smiled tenderly, reaching up to brush a stray lock of brown hair from Lexi's face. "I love you too, Lexi."

At the far end of the room, a small orchestra took their seats, tuning their instruments in anticipation of the night's revelry. The musicians exchanged glances before the conductor raised his baton, and with a single, decisive stroke, he set the music into motion.

The first chords of a waltz wafted through the air, wrapping around the many conversations and pulling them to a close. Lexi and Max exchanged a knowing look, their hearts beating in unison with the melody that now filled the room. They had faced so much together, but tonight they would be swept up in the joy and celebration of their love.

"Shall we?" Max asked, extending her hand to Lexi with a mischievous grin. Lexi's eyes brightened with excitement, and without hesitation, she accepted the invitation.

"Absolutely," Lexi replied, the tone of her voice revealing her eagerness to have this dance with the woman who had captured her heart.

As Lexi and Max stepped onto the dance floor, the elegant swirl of the waltz seemed to surround them, its melody weaving an almost tangible magic between them. Their eyes held one another like magnets, the intensity of their connection sending a shiver down Lexi's spine. She knew they were no longer two separate beings, but rather, two souls dancing in time, connected by the rhythm of their hearts.

They moved gracefully to the rhythm of the music, each step a testament to their unwavering love and devotion. Their bodies swayed in perfect harmony, guided by the gentle pressure of Max's hand on the small of Lexi's back, while Lexi's fingers traced patterns along the contours of Max's shoulder.

Lexi's heart swelled with emotion as she felt Max's strong arms wrap around her, protectively yet tenderly. It was as if nothing could harm her when they were together, as if their love could conquer anything life threw their way.

"Max," Lexi said, her voice trembling with emotion. "I don't know what the future holds for us, but I know that we're stronger together. We can face anything, as long as we have each other."

"Absolutely," Max agreed, her own voice laced with determination. "Whatever comes our way, we'll fight it together. Side by side."

The last notes of the music reverberated through the grand ballroom, signaling the end of Lexi and Max's dance. As they swayed together in perfect harmony, their bodies pressed close, the energy between them was palpable. With each heartbeat, they seemed to merge as one, their love defying the chaos that surrounded them.

The ballroom's grand chandelier cast a warm

glow on the couple, its light reflecting in their eyes as a tender moment passed between them. Some light applause from the dancing guests gradually faded into the background, replaced by the soft murmur of conversations resuming. Lexi and Max stood there, still holding hands, basking in the afterglow of their public spectacle.

"Quite the show we put on, huh?" Max quipped, her smile deepening as she grinned at her partner.

"Excuse me, Lexi?" Marsh's voice sliced through the haze, bringing them back to the present. Lexi turned her attention to the congresswoman, a woman of poise and determination, her dark hair framing a face etched with experience and wisdom. "May I have a word with you?"

"Of course, Congresswoman," Lexi replied, her hand slipping from Max's grasp as she followed the older woman to a quieter corner of the room. She couldn't help but feel a sense of anticipation brewing in her chest, curious as to what the congresswoman wanted to discuss.

"First, I want to congratulate you on your exceptional work for my campaign," Marsh began, her eyes holding a glint of admiration. "Your dedication and passion for our cause have not gone unnoticed."

"Thank you, Congresswoman," Lexi said, feeling her cheeks flush with pride. "It's truly an honor to be part of your team."

"Which brings me to my next point." Marsh paused, her expression growing serious. "I'd like to offer you the position of chief of staff."

"Chief...of staff?" Lexi stuttered, her mind reeling at the unexpected offer. She had always been ambitious, but never imagined that she would be given such an opportunity so early in her career. "I'm honored, Congresswoman, truly. But what about Ethan? He's done an amazing job in that role."

"Ah, Ethan." Congresswoman Marsh gave a knowing smile. "He has indeed been invaluable, but he's moving on to other opportunities. I need someone I can trust to fill his shoes, and I believe you're the right person for the job."

Lexi's mind raced with thoughts of loyalty and respect for Ethan. She considered the weight of stepping into his position and the responsibility it entailed. But she also knew that such an opportunity might not come her way again.

"Congresswoman, I'm truly grateful for your offer, but I need to think about it," Lexi said, her voice faltering under the pressure of the decision before her.

Marsh steadied her gaze on Lexi, the intensity of her eyes urging action. "Lexi, I understand you need to discuss this with Max, but I must stress that time is of the essence. We have a presidential campaign ahead of us, and we need to hit the ground running."

The announcement caught Lexi off guard, her mouth falling open slightly as she processed the unexpected turn of events. The tightness of the revelation settled in her chest, mingling with the already heavy decision of whether to accept the chief of staff position.

"Presidential campaign?" Lexi asked, doing her best to keep her voice steady against the whirlwind of emotions swirling through her mind.

Marsh nodded, her expression serious but proud. "Yes, Lexi. I've decided to run for president, and I believe you have the skills and determination necessary to help me succeed. But we need to move quickly. Our opponents won't wait for us to catch up."

As the congresswoman spoke, Lexi's mind raced with images of what this new opportunity might entail—countless late nights working together, strategizing and crafting speeches, all while navigating the complexities of a presidential race. She felt both excitement and trepidation, the gravity of the situation looming over her.

"Congresswoman Marsh," Lexi began, swallowing hard as she tried to articulate her thoughts, "I'm honored by your faith in me, truly. But I do need to talk to Max first. This is a life-changing opportunity, not only for me, but for both of us."

"Of course, Lexi," Marsh replied, a hint of impatience creeping into her voice. "But please, do not take too long. Every moment we delay is an advantage we give to our opponents."

Lexi nodded, understanding the urgency laid before her. As she walked away from Congresswoman Marsh, her thoughts were consumed by the monumental decision she now faced. She knew that the choice she made would not only affect her future but also the fate of a presidential campaign.

But first, Lexi needed to talk to Max. Their love was her anchor, and they had always faced challenges together. She approached her partner, who stood in the dimly lit corner of the room. Her eyes held a certain curiosity and concern.

"Max," Lexi whispered, pulling her into a tight embrace, "Congresswoman Marsh is running for president. And she wants me to be her chief of staff."

The words hung in the air between them, charged with potential and uncertainty. As Lexi searched Max's eyes for guidance, she found unwavering love and support.

"Let's talk," Max whispered, guiding Lexi to a secluded nook, a haven for the forthcoming conversation about their shared future.

"Lexi," Max began, her voice a mixture of concern and support. "This is huge. But we need to be honest with ourselves about what this could mean for our relationship."

Lexi's eyes met Max's steady blue gaze, and she nodded. "I know, Max. This job would come with long hours, high stress, and constant travel. But it's an incredible opportunity—not just for me, but for Congresswoman Marsh and the change she wants to bring to this country."

"True," Max acknowledged, her thumb gently stroking Lexi's hand. "And I want you to know that I'll always be by your side, no matter what you decide. But are you ready to handle the pressure of being chief of staff for a presidential campaign? Especially when it means putting our plans for the future on hold?"

For a moment, Lexi hesitated. In the back of her mind, she couldn't help but picture the white picket fence and peaceful life she had imagined with Max. But she also knew that she was driven by a desire to make a difference in the world, and now she had been presented with the chance to do just that.

"I need to weigh the pros and cons of this decision. I don't want to make a choice that could hurt us in the long run."

"Let's talk it out then," Max suggested, offering a reassuring smile.

"Okay," Lexi began, taking a deep breath. "On one hand, this job would provide me with an incredible opportunity to make a meaningful impact on our country, working alongside Congresswoman Marsh. I believe in her vision, and I think she has the potential to be a great president."

"Agreed," Max nodded. "And being chief of staff for her campaign would give you the chance to use your skills and experience to help her achieve her goals. It's a big step up in your career too."

"But there are downsides, as I said" Lexi admitted. "The stress, the long hours... I know it would take a toll on both of us. And you're right, we'd have to put our own plans on hold, at least for a while."

Max's expression grew serious as she considered Lexi's words. "It's true that our lives would change significantly if you took this job. But I think we can handle it, Lexi. Our love is strong, and we're both committed to supporting each other through thick and thin. If this is what you want, if you really believe that this is the right path for you, then I'll stand by you every step of the way."

"Thank you, Max," Lexi whispered, tears welling in her eyes. "Your support means everything to me. I just need some time to think it all through before making a decision."

"Take all the time you need," Max said, pulling Lexi into a warm embrace. "I'll be here for you, no matter what you decide."

꙳ ꙳ ꙳ ꙳

Hours later, Lexi stood at the edge of the veranda, gazing out over the moonlit garden. The scent of blooming flowers wafted through the air, a delicate reminder of the beauty that could be found even in the midst of chaos. She took a deep breath, feeling the urgency of her decision pressing down on her like a heavy blanket.

The door behind her creaked open, and Max stepped out onto the veranda, her eyes searching for Lexi's familiar face. "Hey," she said softly, coming to stand beside her. "Have you made up your mind?"

Lexi turned to face Max, her face surely reflecting the uncertainty that swirled within her. "I think so," she murmured, her voice barely audible above the gentle rustle of leaves.

Max reached out and took Lexi's hand, giving it a reassuring squeeze. "Whatever you decide, I'm with you."

"Thank you," Lexi whispered, tears welling in her eyes. "That means more to me than you know."

Taking a deep breath, Lexi squared her shoulders and looked Max straight in the eye. "I've decided to accept the position," she announced, her voice steady despite the nerves that fluttered in her stomach. "I believe I can make a difference working alongside Congresswoman Marsh, and I want to do everything I can to help her win this election."

Max smiled, her eyes shining with pride. "I knew you'd make the right choice," she said, pulling Lexi into a tight embrace. "You're going to do amazing things, Lexi. I just know it."

As they held each other close, Lexi felt a sense of resolve settle over her. Yes, accepting the job would undoubtedly bring challenges and sacrifices, but she was ready to face them head-on, especially knowing that Max would be by her side every step of the way.

"Before we rejoin the others," Lexi said, pulling back from the embrace and looking into Max's eyes. "I want you to know that no matter what happens, I love you. And whatever challenges we face, we'll face them together."

Max smiled, her eyes glistening with unshed tears. "I love you too, Lexi. Always."

Hand in hand, they walked back inside, ready to face the future. For better or worse, their lives were about to change.

Epilogue

The cold wind whipped Lexi's face as she stood on the roof of the glamorous hotel selected for one of Marsh's stump speeches, her eyes scanning the bustling city below. The responsibilities were heavy on her shoulders, but the warmth of Max's hand in hers reminded her that she wasn't alone. They had unwittingly become the face of Congresswoman Marsh's campaign, and with that came scrutiny and challenges they never could have imagined.

"Alright, team," Max said, addressing Hank and Jules, who stood a few feet away, focused on securing the perimeter. "We've got a big day ahead, and we need to make sure everything goes smoothly."

"Copy that, boss," Hank replied, giving Max a salute before returning to his duties.

Max squeezed Lexi's hand, casting a reassuring glance her way. "We've got this, love."

Lexi took a deep breath, her eyes meeting Max's. She knew Max was right—together, they could overcome anything that came their way. "Let's do it."

As they worked side by side, Lexi organizing events and strategizing while Max managed security, their bond grew stronger. Each challenge they faced only served to deepen their connection, as they learned more about each other's strengths and weaknesses.

"Max, I'm worried about the congresswoman's speech tonight," Lexi confessed later, her brow furrowed in concern. "There's just so much riding on it, and I can't help but feel like something might go wrong."

"Hey, Lexi," Max whispered, leaning in close. "I know things are tense, but you're doing an incredible job. I've seen how hard you're working, and I believe in you. We'll handle whatever comes our way."

A tender smile played on Lexi's lips, and she felt her heart swell with gratitude for Max's unwavering support. "Thank you, Max. I don't know what I'd do without you."

"Likewise, love," Max replied, her gaze filled with affection.

As the day progressed, their teamwork was seamless. Lexi would anticipate Max's needs before she even voiced them, and Max was always there to lend a hand when Lexi needed support. They moved in unison, like two dancers who had been practicing together for years.

"Max, we've got a problem," Lexi whispered into her earpiece as she noticed an unruly protester approaching Congresswoman Marsh during her speech. "Someone's trying to disrupt the event."

"Copy that," Max replied, her voice steady and calm. "Hank, Jules, intercept the protester and escort him out."

"Roger that," Hank responded, and Lexi watched as he and Jules expertly removed the protester from the venue, ensuring no harm came to the congresswoman or her supporters.

"Great job, team," Max said, relief evident in her voice.

As the evening wore on and the event drew to a close, Lexi felt a mixture of exhaustion and elation. They had successfully navigated another challenge, and she knew it was all thanks to Max's skill and unwavering support.

"Max," Lexi whispered as they stood side by side, watching the last guests leave the venue. "Thank you for everything today. You were incredible."

"Lexi," Max murmured, her eyes shining with pride. "We did it together. And I wouldn't have it any other way."

❧❧❧❧

Lexi and Max stood side by side, watching the final moments of Congresswoman Marsh's impassioned speech on the large television screen. The atmosphere in the room was electric, charged with anticipation as the results of the Ohio presidential primary were about to be announced. Despite their exhaustion from weeks of nonstop campaigning, Lexi reached down and threaded her fingers through Max's and offered a smile.

"Whatever happens tonight," Lexi whispered, her voice barely audible above the din of anxious murmurs. "We couldn't have done this without you."

"Of course you could've," Max replied, giving Lexi's hand a reassuring squeeze.

As they awaited the results, Lexi's thoughts drifted back to the countless hours they had spent strategizing, organizing events, and working tirelessly alongside their fellow campaign staff. Yet now, on the eve of this crucial event, Lexi couldn't help but feel a gnawing concern in the pit of her stomach.

"Lexi, are you okay?" Max asked as she reached up and rubbed the furrow in Lexi's brow.

"Of course," Lexi responded, offering a weak smile. "Just...nervous."

Before Max could say anything else, the shrill ring of Lexi's phone cut through the air like a knife. Lexi pulled out her phone and saw an unknown number flash across the screen.

"Who could be calling at this hour?" she wondered aloud, her pulse quickening. It might be her mom, calling to congratulate her. No, she would recognize that number.

"Go ahead and answer it," Max encouraged softly, her gaze locked onto Lexi's face, concern etched in her features.

"Hello?" Lexi said hesitantly.

"Hello, Lexi," an ominous voice responded, sending a shiver down her spine. She thought she recognized the voice and felt her breath catch in her throat, her heart pounding. "I hope you're enjoying your little campaign celebration."

"Who is this?" Lexi demanded, clutching the phone so tightly that her knuckles turned white.

"Someone who's been watching you very closely," the man replied menacingly. "And I must say, you've done quite well for yourself. But your success has put you on our radar."

"What do you want?" Lexi asked, her voice trembling with fear as she glanced at Max, who stared back at her with wide eyes.

"Keep your eyes open, dear," the man warned cryptically. "Danger is just around the corner. Good luck, Lexi."

The call abruptly ended, leaving Lexi reeling from the chilling warning. Her hands shook as she looked at the phone, her mind racing to make sense of what had just happened. As she looked over at Max, tears filled her eyes.

"Who was that?"

Lexi's heart hammered in her chest as the sinister voice echoed in her mind, the chilling warning casting a dark shadow over her thoughts. She stared at the phone for a moment longer before her gaze lifted to meet Max's concerned eyes. Her vision blurred with unshed tears as the full weight of the threat settled on her shoulders.

"Lexi, what did they say?" Max asked gently, her hand reaching out to rest on Lexi's trembling arm.

"Someone…someone's been watching us," Lexi whispered, her voice cracking with emotion as she looked over her shoulder at the crowded room. "They said danger is just around the corner."

Max's jaw clenched as she wrapped an arm around Lexi, drawing her close. "I'm not going to let anything happen to you, Lexi." Max motioned Hank over and handed him Lexi's phone. "I want a trace on that last number."

"Sure thing, boss." Hank ran out of the room.

"We need to get out of here," Lexi murmured, burying her face in Max's shoulder as tears spilled from her eyes. "Now."

"We're going," Max vowed fiercely, her grip tightening around Lexi. "Nothing is going to happen."

❧ ❧ ❧ ❧ ❧

As they stood together in the dimly lit office, the night outside pressing in like a suffocating blanket, Lexi couldn't shake the feeling that their world was about to be upended. The anonymous threat loomed over them like a storm cloud, casting a pall over their happiness and leaving them vulnerable to forces beyond their control.

Max's voice cut through the tension. "Let's alert the security team and make sure everyone's on high alert. We can't take any chances."

"Right," Lexi agreed, trying to steel herself against the fear that threatened to consume her.

As they prepared to leave, Lexi paused, staring out the window into the darkness beyond. The city lights twinkled in the distance, but all she could feel was the encroaching danger that lurked just out of sight.

"Max," Lexi whispered as her fingers tightened around the windowsill. "What if we can't stop it? Stop them?"

"Hey," Max said softly, stepping closer and cupping Lexi's face in her hands. "We've faced challenges before, and we've always come out on top."

Lexi nodded, trying to find solace in Max's words, but a cold knot of fear remained lodged in her gut. As they left the room, hand in hand, Lexi couldn't shake the feeling that they were walking head first into a nightmare from which they might not survive.

About the Author

Isabella's first novel, Always Faithful, won a Golden Crown Literary Society Award in the traditional contemporary romance category. She was also a finalist in the International Book Awards, and she received an honorable mention in the 2010 and 2012, Rainbow Awards. Isabella won three Indie Book awards for Faithful Valor and Cigar Barons.

Isabella has written seventeen novels and just finished, Chasing Liberty, a standalone in the strong women that has been in the top five of LGBT drama for six months, with several months at number one.

https://www.facebook.com/isabella.sapphirebooks

or

www.sapphirebooks.com/isabella.html

If You Liked This Book...

Reviews help an author get discovered and if you have enjoyed this book, please do the author the honor of posting a review on Goodreads, Amazon, Barnes & Noble or anywhere you purchased the book. Or perhaps share a posting on your social media sites and help us spread the word.

Check out Isabella's other books

Award winning novel - *Always Faithful* - ISBN - 978-0-982860-80-9

Major Nichol "Nic" Caldwell is the only survivor of her helicopter crash in Iraq. She is left alone to wonder why she and she alone survived. Survivor's guilt has nothing on the young Major as she is forced to deal with the scars, both physical and mental, left from her ordeal overseas. Before the accident, she couldn't think of doing anything else in her life.

Claire Monroe is your average military wife, with a loving husband and a little girl. She is used to the time apart from her husband. In fact, it was one of the reasons she married him. Then, one day, her life is turned upside down when she gets a visit from the Marine Corps.

Can these two women come to terms with the past and finally find happiness, or will their shared sense of honor keep them apart?

Forever Faithful - ISBN – 978-1-939062-75-8

Life is what happens when you make other plans, and Nic and Claire have just found out that life and the Marine Corps have other plans for their lives. Nic Caldwell has served her country, met the woman of her dreams, and has reached the rank of Lieutenant Colonel. She's studying at one of the nation's most prestigious military universities, setting her sights on a research position after graduation. Things couldn't be better and then it happens; a sudden assignment to Afghanistan derails any thoughts of marriage and wedded bliss. Another combat zone, another tragedy, and Nic suddenly finds herself fighting for her life. Claire Monroe loves her new life in Monterey. She's finally where she wants to be, getting ready to start her master's program at the local university, watching her daughter, Grace, growing up, and getting ready to marry the love of her life. What could possibly derail a perfect life? The Marine Corps. Will Nic survive Afghanistan? Can Claire step up and be the strength in their relationship? Or will this overseas assignment and a catastrophic accident divide their once happy home?

Award winning - Faithful Valor - ISBN - 978-1-948232-85-2

Sometimes danger isn't found on a battleground—it's sitting at your front door.

Nic Caldwell is back Stateside, working the job she was supposed to have before her most recent deployment, and living her best life at home. At least she thought she would be, except her PTSD is always in the background, dragging her back to her tour in Afghanistan. As she struggles to control her demons privately, her public life with Claire is almost picture perfect. However, a picture can't show everything hiding just under the surface.

Claire Monroe has the love of her life back in one piece—almost. She's trying to help Nic adjust to her new normal both physically and emotionally while also going back to school and raising their daughter, Grace. With all the difficulties Nic's re-entry poses along with the new challenges of being an adult student, she wonders how she can guide them back to their old life while building a new one for herself.

Cece Ramirez has decided that the Army has served its purpose and she is ready for a new chapter in her professional and personal life. Retiring from active duty and moving on to a new role as a police officer on a college campus, she realizes that she's traded camo, discipline, and rifles for book bags, bikes, and rowdy post-adolescents. While she and the students at Cal State Monterey Bay might be the same age, their pasts are vastly different, and the transition from soldier to college cop may not be as smooth as she hopes.

When a chance encounter at a near-base shopette challenges Nic's authority and leaves her and her family in potential peril, Cece and Claire must pull together to back Nic up in peacetime, and right at home.

American Yakuza - ISBN - 978-0-9828608-3-0

Luce Potter straddles three cultures as she strives to live with the ideals of family, honor, and duty. When her grandfather passes the family business to her, Luce finds out that power, responsibility and justice come with a price. Is it a price she's willing to die for?

Brooke Erickson lives the fast-paced life of an investigative journalist living on the edge until it all comes crashing down around her one night in Europe. Stateside, Brooke learns to deal with a new reality when she goes to work at a financial magazine and finds out things aren't always as they seem.

Can two women find enough common ground for love or will their two different worlds and cultures keep them apart?

American Yakuza II - The Lies that Bind - ISBN - 978-10939062-20-8

Luce Potter runs her life and her business with an iron fist and complete control until lies and deception unravel her world. The shadow of betrayal consumes Luce, threatening to destroy the most precious thing in her life, Brooke Erickson.

Brooke Erickson finds herself on the outside of Luce's life looking in. As events spiral out of control Brooke can only watch as the woman she loves pushes her further away. Suddenly, devastated and alone, Brooke refuses to let go without an explanation.

Colby Water, a federal agent investigating the ever-elusive Luce Potter, discovers someone from her past is front and center in her investigation of the Yakuza crime leader. Before she can put the crime boss in prison, she must confront the ultimate deception in her professional life.

When worlds collide, betrayal, dishonor and death are inevitable. Can Luce and Brooke survive the explosion?

America Yakuza III- Razor's Edge - ISBN - 978-1-943353-81-1

Luce Potter lives by a code of honor. Push her and she shoves back, harder. There's only one problem: Luce has just found out that revenge is a knife that cuts both ways. Now that her lover Brooke has survived the attack on her life, Luce has only one thing on her mind, and his name is Frank. Unfortunately, someone walks into her life that she didn't see coming. Brooke Erickson has survived an attack so brutal it's left a permanent scar on her soul. All she wants to do now is go home and finish recuperating with her lover, Luce Potter, by her side. An unexpected event puts Brooke at the head of the Yakuza family. Can she command the respect necessary to lead it through the crisis? Luce and Brooke's worlds are upending. Can each do what's necessary to survive and return to a new normal

Executive Disclosure- ISBN - 978-0-9828608-3-0

When a life is threatened, it takes a special breed of person to step in front of a bullet. Chad Morgan's job has put her life on the line more times that she can count. Getting close to the client is expected; getting too close could be deadly for Chad. Reagan Reynolds wants the top job at Reynolds Holdings and knows how to play the game like "the boys." She's not above using her beauty and body as currency to get what she wants. Shocked to find out someone wants her dead, Reagan isn't thrilled at the prospect of needing protection as she tries to convince the board she's the right woman for a man's job. How far will a killer go to get what they want? Secrets and deception twist the rules of the game as a killer closes in. How far will Chad go to protect her beautiful, but challenging client?

Surviving Reagan - ISBN - 978-1-939062-38-3

Chad Caldwell has finally worked through the betrayal of her former client and lover, Reagan Reynolds. Putting the pieces of her life back in order, she finds herself on a collision course with that past when she takes on a new client, the future first lady. Unfortunately, Chad's newest job puts her in the cross-hairs of a domestic terrorist determined to release a virus that could kill thousands of women. Reagan Reynolds has paid for her sins and is ready to start a new life. Attending a business conference in Abu Dhabi gives her the opportunity to prove to her father and herself that she's worthy of a fresh start. Her past will intersect with her future at the conference when she accidentally comes face-to-face with Chad Caldwell. Time is running out. Will Reagan confront Chad? Can she convince Chad she's changed, or will death part them forever?

Broken Shield - ISBN - 978-0-982860-82-3

Tyler Jackson, former paramedic now firefighter, has seen her share of death up close. The death of her wife caused Tyler to rethink her career choices, but the death of her mother two weeks later cemented her return to the ranks of firefighter. Her path of self-destruction and womanizing is just a front to hide the heartbreak and devastation she lives with every day. Tyler's given up on finding love and having the family she's always wanted. When tragedy strikes her life for a second time she finds something she thought she lost.

Ashley Henderson loves her job. Ignoring her mother's advice, she opts for a career in law enforcement. But, Ashley hides a secret that soon turns her life upside down. Shame, guilt and fear keep Ashley from venturing forward and finding the love she so desperately craves. Her life comes crashing down around her in one swift moment forcing her to come clean about her secrets and her life.

Can two women thrust together by one traumatic event survive and find love together, or will their past force them apart?

The Gate - ISBN – 978-1-943353-93-4

Valhalla is for warriors that die in battle. What of those who don't have a hero's death? Where do they go? The inter-world is in chaos and has become the heart of the battleground in the war between Paladins and Gatekeepers. Harley doesn't know it yet, but she's at ground zero. A night of drinking, to forget a cheating girlfriend, is about to change her life forever. A birthmark—or a birthright—sets her on a direct path to a woman who claims to have known her for centuries. Not ready to accept her Paladin mantel, she needs proof—and that proof is out to destroy her. A protector by birth, Dawn was bred to preserve the delicate cycle of life and death. Protecting a Paladin is to be mated for eternity, usually without the sex, but Harley's allure is universally compelling. Harley's rise in status to The Chosen complicates things further as Dawn finds herself fighting for her own heart, as well as battling her biggest nemesis and brother, Lucius. Lucius, lord of the Gatekeepers, is out to kill souls moving to their next life. He wants Harley in his corner and he isn't about to let a little sibling rivalry stand in the way, no matter what it takes. Harley find herself caught up in Lucius's tempting promise of power, but cannot shake the soul-tugging love she feels with Dawn. Will Dawn convince Harley in time to embrace her Paladin destiny and save the souls looking for their gate, or will Lucius be able to sway Harley to throw in with the Gatekeepers?

Twisted Deception - ISBN - 978-1-939062-47-5

There are two types of people who can't look you in the eyes: someone trying to hide a lie and someone trying to hide their love.

Addie Blake's life isn't black and white--more like a series of short bursts of color that sustain her until the next eruption. She isn't a ladder-climber in the corporate world. Instead, she works long hours at the office and even at home, something her mechanic girlfriend, Drake Hogan, can't stand. If Addie can't focus on Drake, then Drake finds arm candy that will. After a long week of late nights and a series of text-messaged demands, each one a bigger bomb than the last, Addie has had enough of her Motor Girl.

Greyson Hollister inhabits a world where everything is either black and white, or money green. She's a polished, certified workaholic. As head of Integrated Financial, she has built the ladder others want to climb. Now she intends to attend a business mixer to confront a rumormonger and kill merger rumors involving her company.

Detective Nancy Hill, the lead detective on the Elevator Rapist task force, has just been called in to investigate an attack at Integrated Financial. She can't quite put her finger on it, but something doesn't add up with this latest assault, and Greyson Hollister isn't exactly lending a helping hand.

A storm's brewing on the horizon. Can Addie and Greyson weather it, or will it blow them over?

Award winning - Cigar Barons: Blood isn't thicker than water - it's war! - ISBN - 978-1-948232-83-8

Legends aren't built overnight. In fact, they take decades of hard work, long days, and selfless sacrifice—if one is lucky. Huerta Cigars is a result of the combined passion of patriarch Alejandro Huerta, who emigrated from pre-Castro Cuba to Nicaragua, and his sons Roberto and Manuel. Their unwavering dedication to their dream of producing the best cigars made for a success. Upon Alejandro's passing he left the cigar empire to his only daughter, Sofia, who took over the family business.

Sofia Huerta is Don Roberto's daughter, and she is making a name for herself with her own line of fine, boutique cigars. One late night phone call will change Sofia's life forever. Rushing to Nicaragua from San Francisco, her only hope is that it isn't too late to save her father.

Roberto Huerta, Jr. might be a Huerta in name, but his womanizing, drinking, and carefree lifestyle have kept him at arm's length from his father. RJ think's his father's freak accident will leave him as the rightful heir of the family empire. He couldn't have been more wrong.

A turn of events will pit brother against sister as they fight for control of the Huerta empire. Sometimes secrets and lies aren't the only thing living in the closet, and there is only one Huerta that can continue the family legacy of excellence in this romantic mystery with a twist.

In Cigar Barons, blood isn't thicker than water—it's war.

Dusty Road Home – ISBN – 978-1-952270-72-7

Melanie Crenshaw has fallen off the proverbial map. Notoriously private on a good day, the world-famous mystery author has gone dark to avoid any public blowback or scandal from her latest failed relationship. Seeking quiet and solace, she retreats to her rural hometown, hoping isolation will be just the atmosphere she needs to finish her novel. But going back home is never as easy as it sounds, especially when a nosy reporter starts sniffing around.

Pulitzer-winning investigative journalist Pilar Stein has seen people at their worst—and has the scars to prove it. After taking time off to heal from a particularly brutal assignment, she's back in the saddle and ready to reclaim her place among the elite of hard-hitting reporters. Unfortunately, her re-entry story—a profile on elusive author Melanie Crenshaw who has suddenly disappeared—seems to lack the teeth necessary to catapult her back to the top of her game.

Appearances are deceiving, of course, and Pilar soon discovers that what she deems a simple fluff piece might well lead to the scoop of a generation...just not the one she expected.

As Melanie fights to maintain her privacy while Pilar takes a backhoe to her past, the two women find themselves torn between their own professional convictions and their growing attraction to each other. And no matter which road they take, it's going to be a bumpy ride.

Chasing Liberty – ISBN – 978-1-952270-91-8

Liberty "Libby" Chase's name an explosion of patriotism from her military father and her yuppie, free-loving mother. Her name emerged from a drug-induced haze her parents floated through the night she was conceived. Life threw her a curve ball when she was born with fiery red hair and a too-tall gene, striking an intimidating figure. It's perfect, however, for her personality and for her line of work: a hard-nosed cop with a wicked sense of humor.

Morgan Pierce is a corporate lawyer who has mapped out the path her life will take. So far, it's working out as planned, and she is on track to make partner in her firm. That all-but-certain end is called into question when an unexpected revelation rocks her world off its axis. Perhaps it was inevitable, but now she must come to terms with a lifestyle change that will upend everything—and everyone—in her world.

When a fatal car crash with suspicious origins makes it clear that Morgan's life is in danger, these two women from different worlds must work together to figure out who wants Morgan dead...and why.

Writing as Jett Abbott

Scarlet Masquerade - ISBN - 978-0-982860-81-6

What do you say to the woman you thought died over a century ago? Will time heal all wounds or does it just allow them to fester and grow? A.J. Locke has lived over two centuries and works like a demon, both figuratively and literally. As the owner of a successful pharmaceutical company that specializes in blood research, she has changed the way she can live her life. Wanting for nothing, she has smartly compartmentalized her life so that when she needs to, she can pick up and start all over again, which happens every twenty years or so. Love is not an emotion A.J. spends much time on. Since losing the love of her life to the plague one hundred fifty years ago, she vowed to never travel down that road again. That isn't to say she doesn't have women when she wants them, she just wants them on her terms and that doesn't involve a long term commitment.

A.J.'s cool veneer is peeled back when she sees the love of her life in a lesbian bar, in the same town, in the same day and time in which she lives. Is her mind playing tricks on her? If not, how did Clarissa survive the plague when she had made A.J. promise never to change her?

Clarissa Graham is a university professor who has lived an obscure life teaching English literature. She has made it a point to stay off the radar and never become involved with anything that resembles her past life. Every once in a while Clarissa has an itch that needs to be scratched, so she finds an out of the way location to scratch it. She keeps her personal life separate from her professional one, and in doing so she is able to keep her secrets to herself. Suddenly, her life is turned upside down when someone tries to kill her. She finds herself in the middle of an assassination plot with no idea who wants her dead.

Scarlet Assassin - ISBN - 978-1-939062-36-9

Selene Hightower is a killer for hire. A vampire who walks in both the light and the darkness, but lately darkness has a stronger pull. Her unfinished business could cost her the ability to live in the light, throwing her permanently back into the black ink of evil.

Doctor Francesca Swartz led a boring life filled with test tubes, blood trials, and work. One exploratory night, in a world of leather and torture, she is intrigued by a dark and solitary soul. She surrenders to temptation and the desire to experience something new, only to discover that it might alter her life forever.

Will Selene allow the light to win over the darkness threatening the edges of her life? Two women wonder if they can co-exist despite vast differences, as worlds collide and threaten to destroy any hope of happiness. Who will win?

www.ingramcontent.com/pod-product-compliance
Lightning Source LLC
Chambersburg PA
CBHW031456120626
46545CB00005B/1636

* 9 7 8 1 9 5 9 9 2 9 3 0 7 *